Southern Literary Studies
Fred Hobson, Editor

The Legacy of ROBERT PENN WARREN

The Legacy of
ROBERT PENN WARREN

Edited by David Madden

With an Introduction by James H. Justus

Louisiana State University Press *Baton Rouge* ⚜ MM

Designer: Barbara Neely Bourgoyne
Typeface: Granjon
Typesetter: Coghill Composition Co., Inc.
Printer and binder: Thomson-Shore, Inc.

Dave Smith's essay "Warren's Ventriloquist: J. J. Audubon" previously appeared in *Value and Vision in American Literature: Essays in Honor of Ray Lewis White,* edited by Joseph Candido (Ohio University Press, 1999). Lewis P. Simpson's essay "The Poet and the Father: Robert Penn Warren and Thomas Jefferson" previously appeared in the *Sewanee Review,* 104 (1996). Both are reprinted with permission.

Library of Congress Cataloging-in-Publication Data

The legacy of Robert Penn Warren / edited by David Madden ; with an introduction by James H. Justus.
    p.   cm. — (Southern literary studies)
    Includes bibliographical references and index.
    ISBN 0-8071-2592-X (alk. paper)
    1. Warren, Robert Penn, 1905– —Criticism and interpretation.   2. Southern States—In literature.   I. Madden, David, 1933–   II. Series.

PS3545.A748 Z76   2000
813'.52—dc21   00-028726

In Memory of
C. VANN WOODWARD

Historian active in history

CONTENTS

The essays in this volume represent only a few facets of the legacy of Robert Penn Warren. That most of them deal with the poetry of a writer whose most public image is that of the author of a single novel, *All the King's Men*, only attests to the urgency these poets and scholars feel about the need to call attention to a relatively neglected aspect of Warren's legacy.

If the tendency will be to focus on one aspect, as here, on poetry, or on Warren's fiction, as in classrooms around the country, it may be appropriate and useful to ask whether there is one phrase that captures the essence of the man who has left us such a varied range of works. When we think of Whitman, for instance, the phrases "Oneself I Sing" and "I Hear America Singing" may come readily to mind. Carson McCullers' legacy is to have left us with an understanding of the aloneness of each human being. Faulkner's legacy is the depiction of one region as universal. At a conference in France held to celebrate Faulkner's one-hundredth birthday and to reassess his legacy, a professor from Venice threw out an extraordinarily apt generalization about him in the phrase "myriad-minded." Faulkner certainly was that, and just as certainly, and in many more genre venues, so was Warren.

The writers of these essays speak of Warren in such key terms as "exile," "scholar," "editor," "private person and public life," "mission." "He was a many-sided man," says C. Vann Woodward. "I don't believe I ever knew a more completely fulfilled man." Warren is the exemplification not of the wise and necessary specialist but of the seeker of all knowledge and all forms in which to express it through charged images that ignite emotion, imagination, and intellect. Although none of the writers in this collection uses the term, perhaps Warren is for us the figure of the Renaissance man. In a time when apparently none exists or aspires to exist, it is a distinct pleasure to speak of a writer's legacy as that of a Renaissance man. He shows us what a twentieth-century Renaissance man is like and poses possibilities for writers of the New Millennium in the Internet Universe. The rebirth motif in the term suggests that the "Renaissance man," Phoenix-like, always *is*. There is in each of Warren's works a sense of starting again, and each genre was, for him, a way to start again. We see this rebirth motif in his tendency to revise or recast or re-see key works, such as *All the King's Men*, as verse play, novel, and prose play.

We may say about the Southern Renascence that it is, like most such terms, a loose term that is most useful when used loosely. It is a term that, over time, runs the risk of artificially elevating the minor figures active in the movement and of distracting from the individual achievements of the major figures. Similar cautions may be taken in the use of three other terms applied to movements within the time span of the Southern Renascence: the Fugitives, the Agrarians, and the New Critics. As they apply to Robert Penn Warren, all four loose terms have a limited usefulness for our comprehension of his legacy, now and in the next millennium.

That the question of Warren's legacy came up almost immediately in the year of his death (1989) suggests how clearly what this man created is in fact a major legacy. The strands of many legacies are rewoven in the life, the teaching, and the writing of Robert Penn Warren. We can imagine Dante leading Warren through religion and myth into history; Chief Joseph leading him into the world of the Nez Perce; Thomas Jefferson, himself a Renaissance man, leading him into the vexing ambiguities, paradoxes, and ironies of American history; Audubon and the figure of the hawk (standing for the many birds in Warren's work) leading him into the ambiguous Eden of raw nature; John Brown leading him into the inferno of abolitionist violence; Jefferson Davis, Melville, Whittier, and, as figures of his own imagination, a tormented Southern aristocrat, a New Orleans mulatto, and a Jewish pedlar leading him into descending rings of the Civil War; Hardy and Dreiser leading him into perspectives on the harsh truths of man's condition in the universe and the naturalistic environment man makes; Huey Long leading him into the heart of darkness of Depression political demagoguery; the 1960s African American leading him into the inferno of segregation and desegregation. And we know that

Warren's legacy to us is that, as the figure of the Renaissance man, he in those varied personae led us and leads us still.

Warren's passionate intensity calls to mind at times the Ancient Mariner, leading strangers by the light of his "glittering eye." The legacy of the Renaissance itself comes out, for instance, in his teaching. While teaching at Louisiana State University, he read Dante with graduate student Robert Lowell. Warren was a kind of Virgil himself to many in his various roles. He led Americans into the myriad myths and issues of the Civil War. His first book was a biography of John Brown; he wrote three nonfiction works about the legacy of the war, and in several novels he dealt directly with unusual facets of the war. "The Civil War is, for the American imagination, the great single event of our history," he wrote in *The Legacy of the Civil War*, published at the beginning of the Civil War centennial. "This fact is an index to the very complexity, depth, and fundamental significance of the event. It is an overwhelming and vital image of human, and national, experience."

To those for whom the question of Warren's legacy is important, even—within the literary politics of the day—urgent, "Renaissance man" is word perfect. What is most enduring in his legacy, in the most profound and vibrant sense, in the history not only of Southern but of world literature, is captured in the term "Renaissance man." Who else, certainly among his contemporaries, achieved excellence in such a broad and varied range of genres: poetry, novels, plays, critical works, historical essays, personal essays, biography, and innovative textbooks? Consider Cleanth Brooks, Allen Tate, Andrew Lytle, Caroline Gordon, Faulkner, Welty, Ellison, Richard Wright, Katherine Anne Porter, Peter Taylor, Tennessee Williams, among others. The talent of each is expressed in one salient genre. Warren is in good company with James Agee, Evelyn Scott, and Truman Capote, but it is a small company, and he stands head and shoulders above them. Some would argue his poetry is his greatest legacy and that it will endure. Others will declare that the legacy of *All the King's Men* is most clear. Others may vow that the New Criticism will rise again.

Such claims show that when applied to Warren's legacy, "Renaissance man" is not a glib term. A survey of his life and work in evolving contexts will show that consciously or unconsciously, probably consciously, Warren searched, reached restlessly but with clear vision and intent for ways to express his sensibility, his temperament, his intellect, and that no one genre or intellectual realm could have adequately served his myriad-mindedness. It is quite likely that expression in one genre made work in other genres, if not possible, perhaps richer. Which came first: the novelist's ability to create scenes in the novel *All the King's Men* that could be played out with little change on the stage with great dramatic effectiveness, or the playwright's compulsion to create works in poetry and then in prose for the stage? It was not just an uncanny ability to switch from one genre to another and to do well in each that explains Warren's gift but a fact of temperament that he had an inherent predisposition, which he consciously developed, to respond to the nature and potential of each genre and that movement from one to the other was for him a natural flow of creative energy.

We do well to regard with some complexity the declaration that Robert Penn Warren's legacy is that he was, in a century of increasing specialization, a Renaissance man. But a distinction should be made between the term as applied to Benvenuto Cellini, for instance, and to Warren. Both exemplify the attributes of the Renaissance man in the sense that men in the Renaissance were interested in many aspects of human knowledge, but Cellini worked in only one medium—two if one includes, as one should, his achievement in autobiography—while Warren's distinction is in having taken not only all human knowledge as his province but all genres and modes of artistic expression as his means of pursuing and capturing such knowledge. In our time, the term "Renaissance man" does include the ability to work in many fields and modes. During the Renaissance, few men had that ability; not until Goethe do we see major figures who seek to know everything through every means of expression. Even during the New England Renaissance, Emerson, Thoreau, Melville, Hawthorne, and others were not explorers among genres to the extent that Warren was. Invocation of those names raises the question of greatness. The term "Renaissance man" as applied to Warren, however, is intended to describe his legacy first and only to suggest, second, the level of his achievement.

The critics and poets invited to contribute to this collection of original essays have set themselves the task of assessing Warren's legacy within separate genres. There is a feeling of appropriateness about the fact that this assessment comes a full decade after his death. A safe prediction may be that on the one-hundredth anniversary of his death, when no one work may stand out as monolithically as does *All the King's Men* the term "Renaissance Man" will, as now, set him apart from his contemporaries.

ACKNOWLEDGMENTS

I imagine Robert Penn Warren would have liked knowing that his influence upon my life, my teaching, and my scholarly and creative writing began when I first read *All the King's Men,* while working as a wiper aboard an oil tanker sailing through the Panama Canal in 1952. I'm glad I had the chance to tell him that rereading the novel inspired me to accept the position of Writer in Residence at LSU in 1968 so I could live in Louisiana; coincidentally, he and Saul Bellow awarded me a Rockefeller Grant for fiction that year. The day I learned of his death, I began an effort to commemorate his legacy to LSU and to American history and literature by creating the Robert Penn Warren seminar room in Allen Hall, where he once taught; by seeking funds for a Warren professorship; by putting together a conference on his work; and by inviting contributors to this collection of new essays. I am very grateful to the people who helped me, financially and in other ways, in those endeavors: McMains Foundation, United States Civil War Center, LSU English Department, Robert Penn Warren Circle, Society for the Study of Southern Literature, Random House, LSU's Hill Memorial Library, LSU Conferences; former LSU Chancellor William E. Davis; Maradee Cryer; Dave Smith, coeditor of the *Southern Review;* David Milch and Brandon Tartikoff, former students of Warren at Yale; Catherine Williamson; Tom Turner; Mrs. C. J. Brown; Leah Jewett; Joseph Blotner; Lucy Maycock; Peter Davison; Ellen Bryant Voigt; Shelby Foote; Jay Parini; Betty Adcock; Joe Millichap; Susan J. Moore; my student assistants Lein Shory, Brian Arundell, Manuella Barbuiani, and Lee Ann Alexander; John Easterly, George Roupe, and Fred Hobson, editor of the Southern Literary Studies series at LSU Press.

The Legacy of ROBERT PENN WARREN

Warren as Mentor
Pure and Impure Wisdom

JAMES H. JUSTUS

More than once in Robert Penn Warren's writing occurs the gnomic passage: *nothing is ever lost.* Whatever else the declarative statement may mean, it connotes promise and threat equally—its authority derives from some prior vision presumed to be cohesive, integral, conclusive. More discovery than precept, the statement yet carries the weight of uttered truth. It is what we might expect from a wisdom figure.

If nothing is ever lost, however, it does not follow that everything will be found. In his long career Robert Penn Warren emerges as one of the century's great seekers, and what he found was always more provisional than definitive. The entanglement of will and fate is a given in most of the recording voices we hear in his work—the poetic personae, the narrating protagonists, the reluctant and partial memorist, the amateur historian and sociologist. The writing is a dramatic enactment of a sensibility forever engaged in untangling the relationship of human responsibility to cosmic reality; if the latter remains tantalizingly mysterious, the former is never perfectly known either. The searcher—the yearner—nevertheless plunges on, poem after poem, novel after novel, essay after essay, convinced that patterns of meaning may be discovered and interpreted as entries into the grand secret.

It was Warren's lot—both his fate and his choice—to inhabit the familiar terrain most amenable to the literature of consolation: the pieties of geography and kin, the annals of the poor, the joys of the domestic family, the comforts of childhood, the pride of a national past. Since the mid-nineteenth century, this is a cultural terrain secured by constructions of desire, ranging, we might say, from the mother's knee to Historic Williamsburg—totems that invoke nostalgia and sentimental affirmation. Such artifacts may inspire and assuage, but their major function is to console. As carriers of values they suggest what is lost more than what is saved.

This matrix of conventional consolation literature is also Warren's: the parents as sources of guilt and reconciliation; the hard experience of people on the margins; the love of wife and children; the sounds and sights of nature; recreated scenes from childhood; exempla drawn from prior generations. But in Warren fractious resistances mar such images: wishing the mother dead, scorning the father's compromises, betraying wives and lovers, exposing national predations on Americans of color, locating no confirming meaning in nature, succumbing to the pull of violence. Problems of loyalty (to place, to kin, to friends) and blurred identity recur with disquieting frequency in the half century of Warren's career. The facile cynicism of the early work, derived mostly from his Jazz Age elders, evolved into the probing scepticism of his maturity, in which the intellectual journey for meaning took on an almost visceral intensity. The resources of the search were varied: the bone-and-blood knowledge of African Americans, the canny country lore of the illiterate poor, the testimony of philosophers and prophets, the practical sagacity of forebears, the existential self-spying when immersed in great nature. Warren was a yearner of enormous resilience and patience. Balked and baffled, he forced himself repeatedly into the investigative mode.

But what is most impressive in the persistent tough-mindedness of this long search is the yearner's posture in his old age, where we still find resistance to the easy faith of affirmation, a reluctance to pronounce formulas of consolation. It is easier for the aging writer to accept the culturally proffered role of wisdom figure than it is to decline it. The paradigmatic figures of Wordsworth and Whitman entice all long-living poets, including in our own time Carl Sandburg, Robert Frost, and W. H. Auden. No poet resisted the models more stoutly than Warren. For the artist who, early on, was "willing to go naked into the pit, again and again, to make the same old struggle for his truth," was the same artist who distrusted the "pious truism, fit for sampler work," who retained to the end his own truth that "the hand-me-down faith, the hand-me-down ideals" could be not merely unhelpful but vicious. The quoted passages are from two of Warren's most famous essays, his piece on Conrad's *Nostromo* and "Pure and Impure Poetry." Similar sentiments can be gleaned from the substantial body of his discursive prose. But for my own purposes, I would like to focus on a text that fictionally enacts Warren's interrogative enterprise, one that gives us important anticipatory clues to why this author refused to become the old poet dispensing wisdom.

Consider for a moment "Blackberry Winter," one of the century's great stories and the author's first satisfactory account of how he came to read the world in which he found himself. As we all remember, what is striking in the story is the materiality of a rural world subjected to the caprices of nature. Drowned baby chicks, a dead cow bobbing in a flooded stream, washed-out trash from under an otherwise well-kept cabin are all objects of looming specificity because of a "gulley-washer and a cold spell"—natural phenomena that momentarily disrupt the progression of seasons, creating for the summer-free schoolboy a kind of stasis in which the components of that world stand out, stripped of everydayness, waiting for analysis. The need to know begins with the familiar and the domestic part of that world. The nine-year-old Seth tries to "analyze the tone" of his mother's refusal to let him go barefoot, assessing the "degree of authority and conviction" in her voice; and having gone barefoot, he tries to "read his [father's] face, to see if he was angry." In both cases Seth is unable to decide. He can record but not interpret. We should remember that the narrative perspective here is not that of a nine-year-old child but of a forty-year-old man reimagining his younger self. Because the luminous clarity of the boy's concretely realized world contrasts remarkably with the adult's interpretive perspective on that world, Warren suggests a sobering fact of experience: that to discover meaning in the circumstantial ruck of things is an uncertain process, a program of never-ending reverberations. Indeed, one of the lessons of "Blackberry Winter" is that basic interpretation, the piecing together of the scraps of one's world into a coherent pattern, may take thirty-five years and yet remain provisional.

"Blackberry Winter" turns on the disruption of a comfortable, nourishing, solidly familiar world by a tramp, that fixture of an earlier America. He is the agent of all that is alien—and presumably inimical—to it. Out of an undifferentiated urban world comes this transient—sullen, incommunicative, mysterious, sinister: a naturalistic version of that keening speaker in the old country gospel song who proclaims,

> This world is not my home;
> I'm only passing through.

Although this agent of disruption is ejected by Seth's father, the icon of order, the boy turns from a natural role model to the unlikely other. Seth does not follow his father onto the porch and into the kitchen but follows the defeated tramp up the path—a turn from the comfort, safety, and predictable love of the known to the uncertainty, danger, and predictable hostility of the unknown, from home to the road.

If the nine-year-old boy thinks of the stranger as an unnatural eruption onto his orderly world, the mature narrator knows that he is merely the most startling of sudden reversals created by a nature that flushes the urban stranger into prominence just as she flushes out the trash from beneath Dellie's cabin. The world of "Blackberry Winter" is dominated by an iconography of disruption: a yoked cow, herself yoked to driftwood, clogging a bridge girder; dead chicks strewn haphazardly; flowerbeds inundated by mud, trash, and gravel; a clean yard fouled by filth and debris. These domestic images suggest the fragility of human ordering, but they also serve as visual equivalences of human relationships: a maternal nourisher and friend turn aggressor (Dellie and Little Jeb), and a poor white boy stumblingly betrays his hunger. It is not the intruding stranger but this general disruption that allows "Blackberry Winter" to illustrate one kind of truth: that familial and social understandings are but a thin, easily ruptured membrane over which a civil community moves precariously to avoid drowning in a sea of primal needs. But the stranger so encapsulates that truth that he becomes a shadowy mentor figure teaching certain hard-edged lessons in the reality of going under as well as staying afloat, egoistic assertion as well as disinterested benevolence, death and ruined nurseries as well as tended gardens.

Although Warren restricts his story to a single setting, the pastoral world of boyhood, its particular moment is poised on the point of its dissolution, not because it has already been corrupted (which of course it has) but because violence and uncertainty inherent in that world of apparent innocence have finally staked their claims in the boy's consciousness. Thereafter he will know that the world he walks in consists not merely of what is obviously alien (such as pointed city shoes or a switchblade knife) but country disasters that turn the familiar into the alien (floods, hungry bellies, "woman-mizry," mud that stains like blood, and homegrown versions of apocalypse). "Blackberry Winter" establishes the power of urgencies and yearnings even as it weakens the moral defense erected against them, an aesthetic priority for the dark, subterranean center of experience that will be increasingly felt in Warren's future work.

Mentors by definition are to be followed. The speaker of "Blackberry Winter" records that the tramp commanded him not to follow him; yet he admits, "But I did follow him, all the years." One confirming sign of that admission comes more than three decades later in "Convergences," from *Rumor Verified* (1981). Another Seth, exploring the gorge of a mountain stream, is confronted by another stranger: this time hungry, abrupt, "wolfish and slit-eyed," whose tongue warily slides back and forth. The stranger appropriates the boy's sandwich, bursts his thermos of milk on a rock, and is suddenly gone. But the boy follows him until the stranger becomes "a dot in the distance of sun," disappearing in a railroad tunnel "that sucked all to naught." In this figure, defined as "a man born not to win," a raging deprivation is curiously linked with acceptance, in an uneasy equilibrium that not only suggests the fragility of a world perceived as neatly regulated in its moral and social economy, but also anticipates how the threats to that world are to be borne.

There is another stranger, however, whose presence creates in the boy a kind of casual awe rather than an active threat. This is the tramp of "Dark Night of," another poem of memory in *Promises* (1957). The boy, now twelve, and with a "defective" sense of property, refuses to sic the dogs on an old man, stunned by sun glare, moving tentatively out of the protected darkness of the woods. The young possessor fixes the old dispossessed across a sanitary distance, a gesture sanctioned by country noblesse. Later, near sundown, rounding up the cows, the boy finds the old man crouched amid elderbloom and honeysuckle. Close up, he is "rough-grizzled, and spent," his head "regally wreathed" by white strands; he croaks at the boy ("Caint you let a man lay!"), but resignation is stronger than petulance, and he stirs his old frame and moves off down the lane.

Someone has attributed to Freud the observation that the world is what your neighbors, not your parents, say it is. In the case of the protagonist of "Blackberry Winter" and his avatars in the poems, the world is what both neighbors and a down-at-heels stranger say it is, and the stranger whom the boy follows "all the years" paradoxically becomes a mentor less remote and more ambivalently attractive than his biological father. Because they are loving, the parents are readily and predictably monitory figures; they order, they cajole, they reason with, they advise, they teach. The stranger emerges out of a world unshaped by love, whose lessons are pronounced in sparing croaks, taunts, threats. The stranger is untidy, old (even when the age is vague), grizzled, dispossessed, probably urban; he is enveloped by a private rage whose sources can never be known. The circumstances suggest that *existence* generates rage, explanations for which are hardly capable of being articulated except through weary exhalations, furious exclamations, and expletives that fall staccato-like on the ears of the boy.

The intrusive stranger is a mentor not because of what he says or does but because of what he is. If moral authority is invested, however reluctantly, in such a figure, we should not be surprised at the lack of consolatory wisdom in Robert Penn Warren's later writing. For with the rage to know, to understand, to interpret, what solace can be found in spiritual transience? deprivation and dispossession? restlessness as the moral equivalent of maturity? The stranger is, in a sense, the world's voice, the voice of actuality. But what of the family, the home, the known community? Is there no alternate voice to support the values they are culturally credited with generating—love, charity, responsibility, cooperation?

Yes and no. There is another mentor—a well-known one—in Warren's writing, one who not merely is but says. That figure also appears first in "Blackberry Winter." As the community gathers at the flood-swollen creek to stare at the drowned cow, a poor white boy wonders aloud if "anybody ever et drownt cow"; he is answered by "an old man with a white beard": " 'Son, . . . you live long enough and you'll find a man will eat anything when the time comes.' " Into this garrulousness Warren inserts a crucial detail: " 'Son,' the old man said, 'in my time I et things a man don't like to think on. I was a sojer and I rode with Gin'l Forrest, and them things we et when the time come. I tell you.' " Although the crowd ignores him, he peers at the men and boys "from his weak, slow eyes" and draws his specific experience into an old man's generalization. "Live long enough, . . . and a man will settle fer what he kin git."

What we see here is of course the bare outline of a figure that is to assume much greater authority in Warren's later work. By imaginative assimilation of personal memory into the urgencies of art, this garrulous man craving an audience later metamorphoses into Warren's maternal grandfather, an old man of intense privacies who regales his grandson with war stories and who relives public battles—his grandson as his only audience. The tableau is familiar: the figure of the white-bearded grandfather in blue jeans, smoking his cob pipe or holding it in one gnarled hand, sitting in a split-bottomed chair propped against a cedar tree, occasionally drawing lines with a stick in the dirt to illustrate military battles. Because this recurring tableau is even more personally invoked in numerous interviews, it assumes special status as one of the enabling images of this writer's crucial history.

Although the grandfather, the old Confederate captain who had ridden with Forrest, appears frequently, his function varies. At the simplest level he is a memorial aid to a writer who is convinced that the Civil War is our "only 'felt' history—history lived in the national imagination." As Warren remarked in *The Legacy of the Civil War* in 1961, the memory of the grandfather who had been in the war is a bridge between actuality and myth, a confirming link that indeed makes that war a *felt* history. When in the late 1970s Warren had the opportunity to reassess the Civil War again, this time from a narrower angle, he again characteristically invoked the grandfather: "an old man under the cedar tree, meditating on the past while an ignorant little boy sat there tailor-fashion on the ground." It is the opening image of *Jefferson Davis Gets His Citizenship Back* (1980), and it recurs twice in that slim volume of 114 pages. The book is not about Warren's grandfather or himself as a young boy, but for the first ten pages we are invited to share in a special kind of autobiography—one in which the personal intersects imaginatively with local history, family legend, and the reverberating effects of two wars. "He *was* history," Warren says of his grandfather, which means that he is the personification of national trauma, a reminder of continuities as well as a brooding totem signaling the influence, for good or ill, of the *done* on the *to be done*—in short, a wisdom figure.

But because Gabriel Penn is Robert Penn Warren's grandfather his function as a wisdom figure can never be quite that simple. Warren has spoken of the old soldier as "uncommunicative," leaving us to assume that his stories told to his grandson came sporadically and fragmentarily. The dedication page of *Being Here* (1980) reveals, I think, something of this complexity:

> To Gabriel Thomas Penn
> (1836–1920)
> OLD MAN: You get old and you can't do anybody any good any more.
> BOY: You do me some good, Grandpa. You tell me things.

What are the things the "bookish" old man tells the boy? How important it is to read books and to meditate? The joy of memorizing and reciting poems? The way battles were or should have been fought as illustrated by Napoleon and Nathan Bedford Forrest? Yes: all these things the old Confederate soldier tells his grandson in those lazy summers on an isolated Kentucky farm just before World War I. But in the poems in which he figures, what the old soldier really tells is sometimes frustratingly embedded in what he only partly tells.

"Court-martial," from *Promises,* develops from a chance word the boy hears: *guerrilla.* The old man translates it into a less honorific idiom— "Bushwhackers, we called 'em"—and illustrates the term not with an anecdote or a heroic battle encounter, but a confession. In this story of *guerrilla* war, the old man—"Captain, cavalry, C.S.A."—discriminates among those committed to a cause and those plundering the countryside for their own gain, those whom it became justifiable to kill outright. But for those with a queasy stomach or conscience, the old man mutters, "You could make it all regular, easy," with an impromptu court-martial. The impact of the memory rouses the old soldier out of his serenity, and the queasy stomach and conscience reach out across the years:

> "By God—" and he jerked up his head.
> "By God, they deserved it," he said.
> "Don't look at me that way," he said.
> "By God—" and the old eyes glared red.
> Then shut in the cedar shade.

The grandfather's halting recall triggers the grandson's imaginative re-enactment of the hanging, the captain, now young in his great cavalry boots, riding large in the sky, swinging to the saddle's sway:

> The horseman does not look back.
> Blank-eyed, he continues his track,
> Riding toward me there,
> Through the darkening air.
>
> The world is real. It is there.

The diminution of the heroic comes without judgment, only the stark reality of acts performed and responsibilities assumed. What remains is the human, not the heroic. The felt compulsion to perform an act and the stomach-churning conscience that persists beyond the act coexist, almost as if evaluation were irrelevant in light of the moral tension that we all must live in. What the grandfather loses is the irrefutable status of a conventional wisdom figure, but what he gains is complexity, which for Warren means human frailty acknowledged, a dimension that makes man more rather than less human.

The nine-year-old boy in "The Day Dr. Knox Did It" is hot for certainties in asking why a man would kill himself in a barn with a twelve-gauge shotgun, but the grandfather's responses are unsatisfactory: "It's one of those things," he says, and "Folks—yes, folks, they up and die," and "dying's a thing any fool can do." Even when further pressed, the old man must fall back on: " 'For some folks the world gets too much.' " If the boy immerses himself in a stream hoping that "like water, the world /

would flow, flow away, on forever," he learns only much later that there is "no water to wash the world away."

Even when the old man recurs in *Being Here,* in the volume dedicated to his memory, he is presented not so much as a reservoir of advice, a fount of wisdom to which the inexperienced boy goes for successive draughts, but as a puzzling familiarity, a hieroglyph of which only parts are decipherable. The setting of "When Life Begins" and "Safe in Shade" is the same: the cedar shade, the bearded old man in jeans, one hand wrapped around a cob pipe, his gaze fixed on a mythic distance. What the wisdom amounts to in these poems, behind the heroic charge, beyond the pressure of hunger and thirst, is the incommunicativeness of wisdom.

As generative models, these two recurring figures in Warren's work would seem to occupy opposing extremes. The stranger is the alien spoiler whose chance encounters with the boy are disruptive of a nurturing world of regulated behavior, dependable routine, and predictable human responses. The old soldier is a central representative of that familiar world, a living link between past and present, a symbol of generational continuity and therefore of the values that lend meaning and coherence to life. The stranger takes his definition from the road, the old soldier from the cedar tree. The weary restlessness and hungering mobility of the one counter the stability and serenity of the other.

But in the actual working out of these figures, in their vital engagement in the spiritual drama of Warren personae, the real differences between the stranger and the old soldier seem to fade. If the stranger is an inadvertent mentor, assuming that unplanned role retrospectively, the grandfather's organic function as surrogate father—or better, as parental extension—is translated into something equally unplanned, less protective, less respectful of the Edenic parameters of the boy's home. Paradoxically, under the loving aegis of family the boy learns the actualities of loss, diminishment, pain, guilt; and if these intimations of mortality are less abrupt and harsh than those of the stranger, they are no less chilling to the complacencies of boyhood. Even when the grandfather's words are direct and instructive, as in one of Warren's late poems, "Old Time Childhood in Kentucky," they are less triumphant words to live by than a code of moral minimalism: " 'Love / Your wife, love your get, keep your word, and / If need arises die for what men die for.' "

The grandfather is finally just as inadvertent a wisdom figure as the stranger. Warren's fondness for the doubled point of view device is itself an instructive clue to the writer's moral stance. The self as nine- or twelve-year-old boy—bright, curious, lonely, and hot for certainties—is never seen except through the scrim of the self as man. And, for all his maturity, he is still bright, curious, lonely, and hot for certainties. But what gives depth to the double perspective is the melancholy realization that answers to vital questions we all live with are merely variants of those questions. Human wisdom itself is inadvertent. Like Mercutio and the Nurse in *Romeo and Juliet,* the stranger and the grandfather in Warren's writing shatter the ideal constructions that only the naive and the sentimental believe in. Making peace with Mercutio, these grudging mentors, like impure poetry itself, call the poet back to the marred world of imperfection.

The bracing consistency with which he invoked that world is one legacy of Robert Penn Warren. From the mid-1950s on, that poetic voice sounds like no other. In the very decade when the national culture tapped into the sources of spiritual renewal, civic optimism, and conforming complacency, Warren sounded his bittersweet affirmations and inconclusive yearnings. By the 1970s it became clear that the nagging existential explorations that had become the Warren trademark would never be fully mapped.

If his voice is not the consoling kind, neither is it misanthropic. It is tonic, not sour. What generally protects Warren's vision from helplessness and futility is a kinetic joy, a resilient energy, that lies in the very *struggle* for meaning. In "The Mission," Warren links the circumstantial world, our home that shifts and crumbles over the long ages, to the human species doomed to live in that terrestrial slippage. If the human mission is somehow forgotten, the speaker concludes that perhaps the "lost mission is to try to understand / the possibility of joy in the world's tangled and hieroglyphic beauty."

The premise behind most of the pieces gathered here is the persistence of Warren's own restless mission, manifested in the several genres the writer so adeptly exploited, to plumb the resources of this world for whatever clues that might illuminate his role in it. The stubborn search for his meaning, even when it veered into solipsism, may be the most private kind of wisdom; but Warren never lost sight of the vital linkage of his own yearning to the ongoing human quest for meaning. And however significant as geography, Kentucky and Italy, Baton Rouge and San Francisco, Vermont and Colorado are cartographical markers of a seeker whose boundaries were as flexible as the mission was firm.

The note that *The Legacy of Robert Penn Warren* persistently strikes is the centrality of the writer to twentieth-century American culture. Warren both participated in and lived through the literary phenomenon that we once confidently called the Southern Renascence; and while there is much yet to be learned from assessing the Southern wellspring of his creativity, readers who write about his work no longer feel constrained to reconnoiter Dixie as a cultural prerequisite. In its rich variousness, Warren's career incorporates most of the aesthetic and intellectual schema of our century—although until recently too few critics have sought to explore that richness. In this volume, the very diversity of approaches that we see in Lewis Simpson and Lucy Ferriss, Ernest Suarez and C. Vann Woodward, Victor Strandberg and R. W. B. Lewis assumes the emergence of Warren from a provincial context of feisty Southern modernism (the category that fixed his reputation for years beyond its relevance) to the turf of moral and aesthetic speculation that all great writers claim. To muddy the comfortable assumption that Warren is a Southern poet, as T. R. Hummer and John Burt do, is (not so) simply to draw our attention to the now-obvious fact that the legacy of Warren is something greater than being the second (or third?) brightest light of the Southern Renascence. To attribute the term *moral philosopher* to Robert Penn Warren, as James Grimshaw does, forces us rightfully to imagine a figure transcending the South, a landscape not notably rich in that particular species.

That capacious hunger to transcend both geography and self perhaps accounts for the modesty of whatever wisdom Warren allowed himself. Old poets become beloved only if they sand down their kinks and tics and project themselves as models of consolation. It is to Warren's credit—and perhaps to his readers' as well—that Warren never descended to being beloved. In the last twenty years of his career, he resisted the self-image of the old man dispensing wisdom; what was interrogative and provisional in earlier years remained so to the end.

Robert Penn Warren

Geography as Fate

R. W. B. LEWIS

It was Ralph Ellison who was given to saying that "geography is fate," adapting a familiar formula (about character) to his own sense of things. For Ellison, the fatefulness consisted in having grown up in what was still, atmospherically, a "territory"—Oklahoma, a place of openness and possibility even for an aspiring young black man—and then, moving east, spending his life from his twenties onward in the turbulent, crowded, wholly urbanized world of New York. The contrast between the southwestern territory and the northeastern city, as experienced and meditated, became a source of creative energy for Ralph Ellison; it throbs at the heart of *Invisible Man* and finds expression in many an essay, like the one specifically called "Going to the Territory."

Geography, over the course of time, provided Robert Penn Warren with a similar tension, or dialectic, a comparable source of imaginative creativity. But in Warren's case, the matter was more complex. There was, to begin with, the literal geography of his life, the regions and places he lived in seriatim and sooner or later wrote about. Then there was what might be called the cultural geography, something that developed after the born-and-bred Southerner moved north and east and settled in New England, and taking the form of a Northern-Southern dialectic—as in his book of 1960, *The Legacy of the Civil War*. And beyond that, to some extent evolving out of that, there was a species of symbolic geography, as it were, a geography of mind and spirit. These are the three dimensions of the theme that I would like to consider here.

Geography, as it happens, was important to Warren from his early days. In his teenage reading, as he would say in a 1957 interview, and in addition to such diversely captivating poems as "How They Brought the Good News from Ghent to Aix" and "Lycidas," Warren came upon Henry Thomas Buckle's innovative *History of Civilization in England* (its two volumes published in 1857 and 1861) and was enthralled by it. The "thing that interested me about Buckle," Warren told the interviewer, "was that he had the answer to everything: *geography*. History is all explained by geography. I read Buckle and then I could explain everything."

In the poetry of his prime, Warren set out to explain himself, to himself, via poems that traced his own geography, or better, geographical history. The Kentucky of his childhood and youth, for example, is evoked on several poetic occasions, with titles like "Old-Time Childhood in Kentucky," "Boyhood in Tobacco Country," and "Boy Wandering in Simms' Valley." The latter tells of the boy, Warren, at perhaps age fifteen, clambering up through the brush and love-vine to the top of a ridge and revisiting a scene emblematic of the human lot:

> down the lone valley, called Simms' Valley still,
> Where Simms, long back, had nursed a sick wife till she died.
> Then turned out his spindly stock to forage at will,
> And took down his twelve-gauge, and simply lay down by her side.

This whole area, southern Kentucky southeast to Nashville, Tennessee, was the region Warren loved best. He came back to it rejoicingly in 1931, after the graduate years in California and at Yale and Oxford, to become an assistant professor at Vanderbilt in Nashville. He was ready to settle down forever. "The place I wanted to live, the place I thought was heaven to me after my years of wandering," Warren said to Louis Rubin in a 1977 interview, "was middle Tennessee." He was on the verge of buying a small farm not far from the university, a site where he could live, plant a garden, and write, when he learned that Vanderbilt was letting him go. There was the possibility of a job in Memphis, but that was the wrong part of Tennessee; and then, through the efforts of Cleanth Brooks, Warren was offered a position at Louisiana State University. So he moved to Baton Rouge.

The most immediate product of the Louisiana experience (which ran from 1934 to 1942) was, of course, *All the King's Men,* the novel drawn from the colorful life and the death-by-assassin of Louisiana's governor and senator Huey Long—as Warren said forthrightly to a young friend during the book's composition but was loath to acknowledge in after years. But poetry came out of the LSU days as well, most notably "Folly on Royal Street Before the Raw Face of God," which was contained in the volume *Or Else* in 1974.

It is a lively, multitoned poem that recalls a particular Sunday, say in 1937, when Red Warren and two friends, here identified simply as C. and M., came into town on a bender. (Warren had rented an apartment on Royal Street in New Orleans' French Quarter for such excursions.) The poem begins with a sardonic revision of several lines from Milton's *Samson Agonistes,* then spirals downward into the vernacular.

> Drunk, drunk, drunk amid the blaze of noon,
> Irrevocably drunk, total eclipse or,
> At least, almost, and in New Orleans once,
> In French Town, spring,
> Off the Gulf, without storm warnings out,
> Burst, like a hurricane of
> Camelias, sperm, cat-squalls, fish-smells, and the old
> Pain of fulfillment-that-is-not-fulfillment, so
> Down Royal Street—Sunday and the street
> Blank as my bank account
> With two checks bounced—we—
> C. and M. and I, every
> Man-jack skunk-drunk—
> Came.

The Miltonic lines spoken by blind Samson read,

> Oh dark, dark, dark, amid the blaze of noon
> Irrevocably dark, total eclipse
> Without all hope of day!

The literary point is that not only does Warren's speaker at once rehearse and twist that language (he is irrevocably blind *drunk*), but, starting with that lordly echo, the stanza concludes in the depth of Southern vernacular: "every / Man-jack skunk-drunk." The distance between those two rhetorical levels is akin to what I am calling Warren's symbolic geography.

But to stay with the literal a bit longer: Warren's fateful geography continued when, after LSU stingily refused to meet his modest salary request, he went up to the University of Minnesota, staying there, with interruptions, from 1942 to 1949. From that northlands scene, Warren eventually derived poems like "Minnesota Recollection" and "Minneapolis Story." The last-named, a product of 1980, looks back to a Christmas Eve "Long years ago, in Minneapolis," with the poet, "Head thrust into snow swirl," making his arduous way down a side street, hearing "Church bells vying with whack of snow-chains on / Fenders."

From Minnesota, Warren came to New England as a teacher at Yale from 1950 (with one sizable gap) until his retirement in 1973. Warren and his second wife, Eleanor Clark, divided their family residence between a remodeled barn in Fairfield, Connecticut, and a ranging old house surrounded by woods and a lake in West Wardsboro, Vermont. The Vermont landscape elicited a number of poems, the most winning of them, perhaps, being "Vermont Ballad: Change of Season" in 1980. Autumn is giving way to winter in this sequence of ruminative tercets; "fitful rain" is making "new traceries" down the windowpane, and the outlook is gloomy:

> what do I see beyond
> That fluctuating gray
>
> Last leaf, rain soaked, from my high
> Birch falling, the spruce wrapped in thought. . . .

There is a certain unexpected Southern perspective in the image: only a Kentucky-born observer, one feels, would think that a New England tree, like a New England philosopher, was wrapped in thought. But then, at the poem's end, the Southern viewpoint becomes overt when the speaker sees a man outside

> trudging
> With stolid stride, his bundle on back, . . .
>
> A man with no name, in the gloom,
> On an errand I cannot guess.
> No sportsman—no! Just a man in his doom.
>
> In this section such a man is not an uncommon sight.
> In rain or snow, you pass, and he says: "Kinda rough tonight."

The Southerner-Northerner dialectic (Warren's stretch of cultural geography) had in fact become especially striking some twenty years earlier, in the wake of Warren's early-1950s transference to New England. It almost inevitably took the form of a greatly quickened interest in the 1860s war between the North and South, and it expressed itself most tellingly in two texts of 1960, the book-length essay *Legacy of the Civil War* and the novel *Wilderness,* along with the poem "Two Studies in Idealism" the year before.

Legacy opens with the thought-churning remark that "The Civil War is, for the American imagination, the great single event of our history. Without too much wrenching, it may, in fact, be said to *be* our history." And a little further on: "The Civil War is our only 'felt' history—history lived in the national imagination." It certainly lived in Warren's imagination in these years, and not least in the poems that evoked his grandfather Gabriel Penn, who had been a cavalry officer in the Confederate Army and had ridden with Nathan Bedford Forrest.

> Under the cedar tree,
> He would sit, all summer with me:
>
> .   .   .   .
>
> Captain, cavalry, C.S.A.,
> An old man, now shrunken, gray,
> Pointed beard clipped the classic way,
>
> .   .   .   .
>
> His pipe smoke lifts, serene.

So begins the poem "Court-martial" of 1957, with Warren, entering his fifties, looking back from his New England habitat to those summer afternoons more than forty years before, when Grandfather Penn would reminisce to his grandson about wartime episodes.

As its title indicates, *The Legacy of the Civil War* is primarily concerned with the abiding consequences of the struggle, about which, as the dialectic intensifies, Warren deposes: "To give things labels, we may say that the War gave the South the Great Alibi, and gave the North the Treasury of Virtue." "By the Great Alibi," he goes on, "the South explains, condones, and transmutes everything," everything from lynching to the whole problem of race, which, "according to the Great Alibi, is the doom defined by history—by New England slavers, Midwestern abolitionists," and so on. And then, turning north: "If the Southerner, with his Great Alibi, feels trapped by history, the Northerner, with his Treasury of Virtue, feels redeemed by history. . . . He has in his pocket . . . a plenary indulgence for all sins, past, present, and future, freely given by the hand of history."

Something of that merciless contrast shapes the poem "Two Studies in Idealism," a work that gives us, first, the voice of a Southern countryman killed at Shiloh, and next that of a young Harvard graduate, class of 1861, who apparently does the killing before he himself is shot. The poem's subtitle repeats the opening note of the *Legacy* essay: "A Short Survey of American, and Human, History." This Civil War incident, with the Southerner and the Northerner each having his say, *is* American history in essence, and even an image of all human conflict.

Rhetorically, "Two Studies" reverses the movement of "Folly on Royal Street," going from the most down-to-earth vernacular to the upper-class lofty. The Southerner is remembering the women he has enjoyed: "I reckon I taken my share, / Bed-ease or bush-whack," and his single regret as he dies is that he only managed to kill three Northerners:

> hell, three's all I got,
> And he promised me ten, Jeff Davis, the bastard. 'Taint fair.

The Harvard boy is already enveloping himself in the Treasury of Virtue and the well-stuffed language that goes with it:

> I didn't mind dying—it wasn't that at all.
> It behooves a man to prove manhood by dying for the Right,
> If you die for Right, that fact is your dearest requital.

It only annoys him that Southerners can die, like the man he has just killed, who are not fighting on the side of Virtue.

The novel *Wilderness* brings Adam Rosenzweig, a young Bavarian Jew, to America in 1863 to take part in what he regards as a war for freedom. He undergoes various adventures, both enlightening and disillusioning, is a witness to violence and commits violence, and at the end is perhaps ready to take his full part in the conflict. The work has some handsomely realized moments, such as an account of the New York City draft riots in July 1863, but it suffers from Warren's most dangerous rhetorical tendency—that of drifting toward abstract generalizations. The entire concluding section presents Adam lying on the ground after killing his first Southerner and thinking about the nature of human destiny. He says things to himself such as: *"What I have done I did for freedom. I would have died for freedom."*

The narrative at points like this seems to suffer from the Harvard graduate's rhetorical disease. We can almost hear Adam saying that dying for freedom would have been his dearest requital. For the fact is that Warren both indulged in and attacked and satirized the abstractionist habit. It was the habit he most deplored in Ralph Waldo Emerson, who, Warren contended, was simply out of touch with the actualities of experience; he remained too far above the world. Warren found the perfect metaphor for this judgment in his poem of 1966 "Homage to Emerson, On Night Flight to New York," in which the poet sits in his seat on the plane, heading eastward, with a copy of Emerson's essays on his lap. In the light from overhead, the book's pages seem to say, "There is no sin. Not even error." And within the immediacies of his situation, the poet is almost ready to agree, for

> My heart
> Is as abstract as an empty
> Coca-Cola bottle. It whistles with speed.
> It whines in that ammoniac blast caused by
> The passage of stars, for
> At 38,000 feet Emerson
>
> Is dead right.

Elsewhere, Warren argued that "Emerson cancels evil out of the human algebra" and says that he, Warren, felt a "pathological flinch from . . . these oversimplifications . . . of the grinding problems of life and personality." And yet, as you look closely at these contentions, you feel that Warren is talking to himself. In Warren's attitude toward Emerson, we have, I suggest, a classic example of what Harold Bloom calls the anxiety of influence. Warren's hostility to Emerson's teachings was heartfelt, but what he most disapproved of in Emerson was what, in part of him, he knew was a habit of his own mind: the congenital push or leap into the abstract.

This is, as well, the domain of Warren's symbolic geography, and it was never given finer utterance than in the poem of 1975 "Evening Hawk." The very language of the poem echoes Warren's strictures on Emerson. The poet, probably in Vermont, watches the hawk soaring, like Emerson, far above the human world:

> Look! look! he is climbing the last light
> Who knows neither time nor error, and under
> Whose eye, unforgiving, the world, unforgiven, swings
> Into shadow.
>
> .   .   .   .
>
> If there were no wind, we might, we think, hear
> The earth grind on its axis, or history
> Drip in darkness like a leaking pipe in the cellar.

Warren's symbolic geography reached from those remote altitudes, and the language suitable to them, down to the turning, grinding, darkening earth with its own vernacular.

One of Warren's last poems, a Warrenesque sonnet called "Mortal Limit," traverses just that distance. Here the hawk, so apt a symbol for the unfettered mind or imagination, is riding the skies above the range of Tetons in Wyoming. Observing it, the poet gives voice to a fellow feeling of exultation at the new heights the hawk may be achieving, the new vistas he may be seeing. But the poet knows, or such is the implication, that the hawk must finally return to earth, even as the human mind must always do, down into the welter of the here-and-now and the darkness of human impulse:

> I saw the hawk ride updraft in the sunset over Wyoming.
>
> .   .   .   .
>   Beyond what height
>
> Hangs now the black speck? Beyond what range will gold eyes see
> New ranges rise to mark the last scrawl of light?
>
> Or, having tasted the atmosphere's thinness, does it
> Hang motionless in dying vision before
> It knows it will accept the mortal limit,
> And swing into the great circular downwardness that will restore
>
> The breath of earth? Of rock? Of rot? Of other such
> Items, and the darkness of whatever dream we clutch?

Exile at Yale

C. Vann Woodward

The title I have chosen for my contribution to our tributes in honoring Robert Penn Warren illustrates too well the shortcomings of short titles. The word *exile,* for example, is burdened with harsh connotations in English as well as American usage. While definitions in the best dictionaries of both countries permit a voluntary meaning for the word, both make that usage secondary and give priority to the involuntary meaning—banishment, compulsory eviction from one's native land. I have no trouble with calling the South Warren's native land. It is the banishment part that is troubling, though I retain it for reasons I hope to explain.

But then to say exile at *Yale* suggests a geographic limit to his exile—however defined—that is too narrow. Warren did spend the last thirty-eight years of his life associated with the university in some degree or capacity—on the faculty from 1951 to retirement in 1973. And in his remaining sixteen years his personal, social, and intellectual life continued to be generously shared with the Yale community. If all years absent from "native land" are included, however, they began twenty-five years before he joined the Yale faculty. After graduating from Vanderbilt he spent four years, *Wanderjahre,* as student at California, Yale, and Oxford. In a later interview he said, "Something happened to me at Oxford that simply took me back to the South." It was more a compulsion than a choice. "I had to go back," he said, and repeated, "I just felt I had to go there . . . so I came back from Oxford and became wedded to the South again."

While he felt he "could have gotten a bad job elsewhere," he accepted an offer to teach as a junior professor at Southwestern College in Memphis for one year and next at Vanderbilt for three years. Only then, in 1934, when Louisiana State University offered him attractions that included congenial colleagues and wider intellectual opportunities, did the wandering poet, scholar, and teacher appear to have found permanent roots in his beloved native land.

Yet of course we know, though he did not until later know, that his wanderings were not ended. I am very reluctant to jump to any conclusion about why Warren departed LSU for exile in Yankeedom after only eight years there, the more so because of the numerous and credible reports of his brilliant achievements and soaring reputation during those years. The spring after his arrival in Baton Rouge in the fall of 1934 at the age of twenty-nine he organized a conference of many friends to help with the plans for a new literary journal. His first volume of verse in 1935 came out the same year that the first issue of the *Southern Review* appeared. His friend Cleanth Brooks from Vanderbilt and Oxford days was coeditor, and Albert Erskine, who became Warren's editor at Random House in later years, was business manager.

The success of the new journal was phenomenal. In its pages appeared a flow of first-rate literary talent, Auden, Eliot, Huxley, five stories by Eudora Welty and several by Katherine Anne Porter, as well as many newly discovered writers with their first poem or story in print. The *Southern Review* was a conspicuous feature of the ongoing Southern Renascence. Its very title, the editors said, was an expression "of the regional and sectional piety of the editors." Among literary circles on the Hudson, Baton Rouge was sometimes referred to in those days as Parnassas on the Mississippi. Editor Warren also won distinction and much satisfaction as teacher Warren at LSU. Among the graduate students he attracted and taught was Robert Lowell, who was to become one of the most famous American poets of his time. Mentor and pupil would sit and read Dante together in Italian for two hours several days a week. Lowell's wife Jean Stafford became secretary of the *Southern Review*. Lowell said that as a student he would "listen to Robert Penn Warren talk for hours about

Machiavelli, Cesare Borgia," and years later he exclaimed over a Warren poem, "An old master still engaged the dazzled disciple."

What more could a dedicated young southern literary critic, poet, novelist, teacher, scholar need than what he had at LSU to bind him to a place and an institution with bonds of loyalty and gratitude? All this he had, and if that were not enough, he had in addition a home sufficiently remote from the campus to assure him the privacy a writer needs, as well as the metropolitan attractions of nearby New Orleans, with the art colony and writers it attracted.

Yet in spite of all this we know that after eight years, with a Great Depression not yet ended and a great war not yet won, Warren picked up and left in 1942. He resigned his chair at LSU, but this was more than a resignation. It was the beginning of his life in exile from his beloved native land. Whether he thought of it that way then I do not know. Nor, for reasons already mentioned, will I guess his real reasons for the decision. I know, of course, that the explanation most commonly heard was the suspension of the publication of the *Southern Review* by an order of the president of the university in 1942. And I have heard several explanations of that action, including the hostility of several faculty members and the feeling of certain administration officials that the university could not afford such a "luxury" in wartime.

Though I never heard Warren say so himself, it is commonly believed that he resigned with the feeling that he was not understood or appreciated or sufficiently welcome. Louis Rubin quotes him as saying in 1977, "I wanted to live in the South, you see; I'm a refugee from the South, driven out, as it were." He found LSU "a very exciting place," he said. "And I left Louisiana only because I felt I wasn't wanted. I felt pressure to leave. It wasn't a choice. I had settled down . . . settled down for life, I assumed. I left, shall we say, under pressure of some kind or another. I wasn't fired. I left out of pride." I find it hard to dismiss the suspension of the *Southern Review* as an important factor. But there could well have been other reasons. Such events often have more than one cause. A failed first marriage, for example. Or the appeal of an attractive offer from a distant and distinguished university. And one should not forget the wild restlessness that in 1942 was spinning Americans all about the globe, some of us in military uniform. No university can accept responsibility for such things, and yet they can influence profoundly university decisions, losses, policies, and institutional reputations.

Whatever the cause and wherever the responsibility lay, his departure in 1942 at the age of thirty-seven marked the beginning of Warren's exile that lasted the remaining forty-seven years of his life—eight of them at the University of Minnesota and the rest at or around Yale.

Thinking of Warren as a writer in exile suggests comparisons with three famous writers of his time or a bit earlier to whom the term *exile* is often applied. I am thinking of James Joyce, Ezra Pound, and T. S. Eliot, all exiles of some sort, but each in his own way and each for his own reasons. Lewis Simpson mentioned Joyce in this connection several years ago. Joyce left his native Ireland in his youth and lived abroad the rest of his life, yet all his great works are about his provincial native land. Pound, a native of Idaho, spent nearly all his adult life in Italy, England, or France. His prolific writings, however, contain little of note about his native land save his identification of Jefferson with Mussolini and his Fascist propaganda during World War II. For that he was returned to America to face trial for treason but was instead committed to a mental institution. T. S. Eliot, a native of St. Louis, carried his exile to the point Henry James had before him by becoming a British subject in 1927 and still further by changing his religious affiliation. Reasons for their decisions to resort to exile were probably as varied, obscure, and complex as the pattern of exile they experienced, which took many different forms.

Unlike Joyce, Warren did return to his native land, if only for visits and because of family ties, but never again to settle and live there. He felt a strong relationship with the Irish, he said, "particularly the Irish because ours is a provincial area, speaking provincial English." And like Joyce he wrote almost exclusively about the people and culture of his native province. The only exception that comes to mind is his narrative poem *Chief Joseph*. But as Warren said, "poetry is different from fiction," and his poems take settings in many countries. It never occurred to him, he told Ralph Ellison in reference to fiction, that he "could write about anything except life in the South." And to a remarkable extent the events that inspired him, he said, occurred "around my home, that part of Kentucky," or Tennessee, a hundred yards south of his birthplace, or still further south.

Unlike Ezra Pound, who became alienated from his native land during his exile to the point of treason, Warren maintained a strong identity with the South, though, he said, with "no romantic notions about it." He deplored and opposed and spoke out often against injustice and oppression and brutality in the South all the more because of his powerful regional identity. He was no apologist, nor was he anti-Southern. In his novels and poems that deal with events or ideas over which Southerners were deeply divided, as frequently was the case, Warren or the fictional characters who served as the narrators typically refrained from taking sides and for the most part remained cool observers. The author himself had differences with his home region, but nothing that could be properly called alienation. On the other hand he never committed himself unreservedly to any Southern cause, or any ideology, including Agrarianism—detachment more than commitment. He repudiated an early essay on race relations. His approach toward the South was less an embrace than a brooding wonder and fascination.

T. S. Eliot's experience and literary uses of exile differed greatly from those of Warren. Eliot did not write about his provincial region or his native country but about his times, the times of Western culture and the life it then fostered. That life he tended to picture as sordid, ignoble, even stultifying. Warren was an admirer of Eliot's work, and his own writings frequently dealt with sordid or ignoble themes, but he would appear to regard these as human weaknesses rather than products of world crisis or the decline of the West.

On the effect of exile upon writers one other comparison, this one with William Faulkner, seems natural, though it might more accurately be called a contrast than a comparison to Warren. Faulkner could not be called an exile in any sense of the word. He remained rooted in his native Mississippi, in one county thereof best known abroad as "Yoknapatawpha," the name he gave it himself—his "postage-stamp of a county," he called it. His absences were prompted by necessity rather than flight—for example those in Hollywood to stave off bankruptcy or the trip to Stockholm to receive the Nobel prize. Otherwise he usually stuck it out in his provincial "postage stamp."

The contrast with Warren in this regard is obvious enough, but the similarities in their writings despite the contrast are less obvious but more important. The exile like the homebody devoted his fiction all but exclusively to subjects peculiar to his native region. In this respect Faulkner was more narrowly focused geographically than Warren. Fourteen of Faulkner's nineteen novels, in fact, including his greatest ones, were centered on his one mythic Mississippi county, and all but one of the others on other parts of the lower South. While Warren, as we have seen, most often chose subjects in the vicinity of his native Kentucky village, he ranged more widely in geography than Faulkner, though in all but one work sticking to the South. His best-known novel, *All the King's Men,* is centered in Louisiana.

One can only speculate on what difference, if any, it would have made in his writings had Warren followed Faulkner's example and resisted exile. Faulkner once wrote with regard to his own work that "this is not the world that William Faulkner created; it is, rather, the world that created William Faulkner." Warren as writer was in this sense also created by his native Southern culture, though not with the concentration and exclusiveness the creator lavished upon the Mississippian.

I must remind myself at this point of the title that I originally chose for these remarks, "Exile at Yale," and the so-far postponed or neglected obligations that title suggests. It happens that I can write with more assurance about the Warren of those years, for I shared most of his exile in close and personal terms. He joined the Yale faculty ten years before I did, but we had met some ten years before that in California and at various places afterward, including Johns Hopkins, where I had arranged for him to speak. I still own and cherish a first edition of *All the King's Men* that he sent me.

When Yale sought to persuade me to leave Hopkins, they enlisted help from Warren. He called and invited me and my wife to a party at his home in Fairfield while we were looking over the situation at New Haven. At the Warrens' party were assembled fellow Southerners to assure me that I would not feel too lonely in Yankeedom. There I was delighted to meet another LSU fugitive, Cleanth Brooks, for the first time, and to see Bill Styron and other Southerners I had known before. More than any one thing, that part persuaded me to pull up roots two years later at Hopkins, where I had long been settled happily and I thought permanently, to move north.

Thereafter I always felt warmly welcome at the charmingly rambling house the Warrens created out of a substantial old barn in Fairfield or the very modern summer house they built in Vermont. Visiting in both regularly I met not only writers and scholars from the South, black and white, but their counterparts from New England. No matter how busy he was in these furiously productive years, Red seemed always to have time for a chat or a lunch or to read and thoughtfully criticize my writings then in progress. I may have become a nuisance at times. But nevertheless he could say in a letter ten years ago, "I am somewhat older than you, but in a way our early lives were almost parallel in various ways. In one way or another, allowing for differences, our situations were remarkably similar. . . . The relation, that is, to the worlds in which we grew up . . . and my (late) passion, that's the word, for reading American history."

I will try to say what I could make of the effects of this long phase of his exile upon Warren's personal life and his writing. On the personal side I cannot help but think of the contrast between the happiness of Warren's experience and the miseries of two of the writers with whom I have compared him earlier—Ezra Pound, who carried his exile to the point of alienation and treason, and Faulkner, who rejected exile and stayed home to endure his pathological addiction to booze and the trials of a very troubled marriage.

Warren's life in exile was blessed by what he pronounced "a very happy marriage in process after a period of an unhappy one and the stopgaps in between." His second wife was the writer Eleanor Clark, "as Yankee as they come," declared Red. Asked if she would change anything in her career if she could, Eleanor replied, "I'd have married him earlier." She bore him two children, both born with gifts of their own—Rosanna, a poet, and Gabriel, a sculptor. Would their father's personal life have been any happier had he never become an exile? It is, of course, impossible to say, but I find it difficult to imagine.

Then there is the question of his new academic life. He no longer had to teach for a living. "But I discovered that I enjoy teaching," he said. "I quit teaching entirely three times but always drifted back in." He never taught more than one term a year and then only two days a week at Yale. But he needed "to keep in touch with the young," and, he added, "When I'm not teaching, I miss it very much." There were not only devoted and brilliant students, but in his words, "Also, you can find in the academy certain people that you can't find outside. There are not too many, but there are some—the real humanists—brave men who love their learning and who love ideas." They were an essential part of his social as well as his intellectual life.

And finally, there is the creative life of the exile as poet, novelist, and I would add, literary and social critic. What bearing did exile have upon all that? Upon Warren the novelist I think of the relationship as somewhat paradoxical. He once said, "The farther I got away from the South, the more I thought about it." Walker Percy has commented on that question for writers of his time. "Indeed," he wrote, "more often than not, it is only possible to write about the South by leaving it." He then pointed to the writers of other regions: "Hemingway in Paris and Madrid. Sherwood Anderson in New Orleans, Malcolm Lowry in Mexico, Vidal in Italy, Tennessee Williams in Key West, James Jones on the Ile de St. Louis in Paris." As for Percy himself, he strongly preferred to live and to work in the South, and after some wanderings he settled in Covington across the lake and did his major work.

Certainly Warren's prolonged absence did not divert or distract him from the subject that remained to the end the central focus—concern, absorption of his fiction with his native region and its people. Any place, on the other hand, might inspire his poetry. As for his literary criticism, he said, "I'm just not a professional critic. That business is just something that happens. . . . But writing fiction, poetry, that's serious—that's for keeps." Yet he continued to be regarded as an important literary critic, and, I would add, as a social critic, a calling that took him back South and was expressed in his deeply felt books on racial segregation and the views and aspirations of black leaders of his time. He was a many-sided man.

We once stood on the shore of a Greek island in the Aegean. Without

addressing anyone in particular he suddenly broke a long silence by saying, "I'm so happy, so happy." With that he stripped quickly and plunged
into the sea. He swam out of sight and remained out of sight for quite a
while. He was still in his prime then and a good swimmer, but I asked
Eleanor if she was not worried. "Oh no," she said. "He loves to compose
poems while he is swimming." I don't believe I ever knew a more completely fulfilled man.

Christ, Start Again

Robert Penn Warren, a Poet of the South?

T. R. HUMMER

I find it interesting and strange to explore the Southernness (of all things) of Robert Penn Warren (of all poets). In the first place, Warren's Southernness may at first glance appear—as it did to me when I first began thinking about this subject—so self-evident that any discussion along these lines would have to be tautological and therefore boring. It is certainly no problem, for anyone interested in doing so, to claim Warren was a Southern poet. He may not be from the South, exactly, Kentucky being a border state (and I for one am not eager to get into any argument, especially with Kentuckians, over whether Kentucky is or is not Southern in fact or spirit)—but his connection with the Fugitives and his founding of the *Southern Review* would appear immediately to certify him. One of the uninteresting ways to frame this discussion would be to rehearse those well-known facts and be done with it. Another would be to approach the poetry itself in a more or less statistical way and prove that 51.24 percent of Warren's poetry is of, for, or about the South. Yet another would be to put forward a number of themes, techniques, images, tonalities, or what have you as belonging specifically to Southern poetry and go on to demonstrate that 51.24 percent of Warren's poetry possesses those qualities. Then we could spend all day arguing about whether those themes, techniques, images, tonalities, or what have you are really Southern, or are only Southern, and whether Warren's poetry really possesses them. This might be amusing, but my experience tells me that in the end it would get us nowhere.

My first impulse, in all honesty, is to wonder just how much the "Southernness" of Robert Penn Warren really matters. It is tempting simply to say that it does not matter at all and then pass on. But this response, no matter how much it appeals to me personally, is as bad as baldly saying "Of course Warren is Southern." The only intellectually decent way to solve the problem "Robert Penn Warren is/is not a Southern poet" is to define the terms. "What is the South?" is a familiar enough question at conferences on regional writing. But if we ask this question, are we not equally obliged to ask, "Well, but what is a poet?" And worst of all, "What is Robert Penn Warren?" I propose to answer all these questions in an alarmingly small number of words.

Anyone who has spent time in the South has seen the bumper sticker that says, "American by Birth; Southern by the Grace of God." Therein lies one kind of definition of the South: an attitude.

Daniel Patrick Moynihan has recently made a telling distinction between *states* and *nations,* a state being a social organization to which one belongs by political fiat, a matter of boundaries, compromises, and laws, and a nation being a group larger than tribe or family, often an ethnicity, to which one belongs by birth. These definitions fit neatly in many parts of the world where one finds states that are comprised of many nations, or peoples who are strangely divided from one another by the artificial action of politics, or ethnic groups entirely deprived of homelands in which to create their own states. The history of the United States strangely subverts this formula: we call ourselves a nation comprised of many states, and we try as hard as we can, much of the time, to ignore the distinctions and differences among the various peoples who comprise the realm. The famous bumper sticker cited above is a symptom of this subversion; Moynihan might revise it to read "Die-cast American by accident; born Southern by the force of history."

American regions occupy a particularly anomalous position in this structure—neither states or nations in fact, they are the ghosts of both. The word *region* derives from the Latin word for *king.* American regions generally, and the South particularly—insofar as the South is the only American region I know of other than the region of Utah which after the thirteen original colonies sorted themselves out still proposed to be its own separate country—are a symptom of the American desire to have everything both ways at once. We are, as the man says, "one nation under God"; we are a vast plurality; we are a number of phantom kingdoms at odds with one another. Even within the peculiar American nesting of differences, the South contains its own rupture, the breach between the races—and though the whole earth suffers from racial tension, the South makes a mysticism of racial difference that is like no other: an attitude.

One may say with truth and justice that any region is simply a place wherein women and men carry on their lives, walking their distinctive walk, talking their idiosyncratic talk—but it is also true that that walk and that talk come from somewhere. That *somewhere* we can sum up under the heading of the single word *history*. A strongly discrete region like the South is the shade of a stillborn body politic, the wraith of a state that might have been, the itchy whisper of a realm of possibility terminated by circumstance, the echo of an alternate reality in the manner of *Star Trek* wherein things that might have been carry on a dim existence in spite of "actual" outcomes, in spite of circumstances, in spite of old bloodshed and battles lost, in spite, in spite, in spite. Regions are twitchings in the amputated ghost limbs of history. White Southerners, as Southerners, go on like Hamlet searching for the body of the murdered king and mourning.

Nobody knows what a poet is, and everyone does. The history of criticism is in no small part a junkyard of attempted definitions of the poet, the artist generally—each of which forms its own region in the life of writing, its own ghost kingdom. For present purposes, we can get off the hook pragmatically and decorously by using Warren's own acute observations on the subject. In *Democracy and Poetry,* for instance, he asserts that "poetry—the work of the 'makers'—is a dynamic affirmation of, as well as the image of, the concept of the self" and that "the 'made thing'—the poem, the work of art—stands as a 'model' of the organized self." Warren, of course, is not so naïve as to assume that the poet is a more or a less "organized self" than other people; often highly disorganized, he tells us, the poet projects *an image of the concept* of an ideal self out toward the future. I repeat, for the sake of emphasis, that deep regression: an image of the concept of an ideal. As for the self itself, Warren maintains that it "is never to be found, but must be created, not the happy accident of passivity, but the product of a thousand actions, large and small, conscious or unconscious, performed not 'away from it all,' but in the face of 'it all,' for better or for worse." And if all this begins to sound a little cozy, he goes on to tell us that "what poetry most significantly celebrates is the capacity of humanity to face the deep, dark inwardness of our nature and our fate," and of poets themselves he says that "the artist may be regarded as the man [or woman, I would add] who cannot project outside himself the 'shadow' self, but must live with it." These ideas are provocative, Warren knew, precisely because they are incommensurable. Together they point toward certain fundamental problems in American art, in the fabric of America itself, that lie in the basic paradox of the attempt to make not merely a state but a nation of utterly sovereign individuals. This is the central problem not only of *Democracy and Poetry* but of Warren's whole enterprise as a writer. Poetry, he says, is an enterprise "in which the doer pursues the doing as a projection of his own nature upon objective nature, thereby discovering both the law of the medium in which he chooses to work and his own nature." Whether or not this is universally true, Warren believed it. Therefore, we can only look for the keys to his enterprise within the enterprise itself.

Some years ago when I was in my mid-thirties, a friend and fellow poet said to me, "Do you realize that if you wrote and published a book a year for the next thirty years, you would not equal the output of Robert Penn Warren?" It was the truth, and it was appalling. As we know, Warren's output was enormous, even prodigal; whether we choose to speak of his gift, his energy, his tenacity, his breadth, or his obsession, we are forced to acknowledge that at least in sheer bulk it is beyond the reach of most mere mortals. His work comprises a large and plural literary region, a sort of kingdom. And insofar as Warren has now, for most of us, gone to live entirely inside his books, he is the shadow monarch of all he chose to convey.

He was, as a matter of fact, a sort of king in life—or at least a literary patriarch. I know a story—perhaps apocryphal but nonetheless true to the image—about Warren's giving a reading at a university where most of the audience consisted of undergraduates. Looking out at them, Warren reportedly said, "I'm delighted to see so many young people in the audience tonight. I am the father you all want to kill." Beyond some more or less undefinable moment in his life and in his career, Robert Penn Warren became surely one of the fathers. Arguing against the American tendency to erase history, Warren wrote in his essay "The Use of the Past" that "we live in a 'society without fathers.' " He is talking about our ethos, not our sociology. The patriarchs, to Warren, are the keepers of the lessons of the past, as well as the past's enforcers; their mortmain is heavy, but it cannot be safely ignored. America, he knows, has tried to do away with its patriarchs and all they stand for, and for good reason: that kind of hegemony is largely incommensurate with democracy. But, he believes, there is a stiff cost for this erasure, and the danger, as he sees it, is great.

If we combine this image of the patriarch with the image of the poet described above, we come up with a creature precariously balanced between past and future—a sort of emptiness (insofar as the self is no more than what we make of it) poised between a horrendous and leaden but inescapable and necessary history and a future that is an abyss. This is no new idea—it would have seemed downright homey to the Greeks—but Warren's rerendering of it is particularly harrowing. His universe is brutal and beautiful; his humanity is heroic but foolish and doomed. The past is unknowable but we have to know it; the future is unforseeable but we have to create it. Warren readers, and especially Warren scholars, know all this very well. Warren makes it clear over and over again; in "The Use of the Past" he puts it this way: the fate of humanity "is double, an outer and an inner fate, the world that the self is in, and the self that is a world. And more and more we see, painfully, that the two worlds are indissolubly linked and interpenetrating—mirror facing mirror, as it were—and more and more we see that one of the errors of the past, an error from which we must learn, has been to treat them as though each were in isolation." What I want to emphasize here is that this terrible and incommensurate and numinous universe limned with increasing clarity in the poetry especially, right up until the end of his life, is Warren's own region, his kingdom. It is a hell of a place, but it is *his* place, and he makes it immense and dignified.

It is precisely here that I begin to discern the core of Warren's debt, and his attachment, to the South. A region with an attitude is inevitably going to be conservative in certain ways—it is the past, after all, tradition, that makes the South the South and makes it different from New England, say, which has its own distinct past and its own brand of conservatism. Marshall McLuhan somewhere points out that regions possess "an unconscious preference for a local and limited point of view." I would say that the preference on the contrary often is absolutely conscious. The region (not to say all its individuals) must go on living in the past and simultaneously in the virtual reality of the destroyed future of which it is the ghost. Otherwise, it ceases to be a region. At the same time, it must negotiate the actualities that surround and permeate it in any given present; otherwise it will be overwhelmed. So the New South negotiates with the Old South and with contemporary Manhattan, Paris, and Beijing. So, too, in the '50s and '60s when I was growing up in Mississippi, it negotiated perforce with Washington and with its own disenfranchised African American population. It was just at that juncture that certain falsehoods in the sovereign mythos of the white South and the "image of a concept of an ideal self" began to come apart at the seams. But the white South, of course, is far from the only South. The righteous demand, then as now, is that the old image of a concept give way to a new reality, a body politic capable of genuine incorporation of all its constituent citizens.

And Warren? How did this paradigm shift, if that is what it was, affect him, and he it? For if indeed he was in any way, shape, or form "Southern," if his selfhood as a white male, a patriarch, was in any real way implicated with the fabric of twentieth-century southern culture, then events in the South just past mid-century must have had their impact on him and on his practice as a poet. If we can gauge the extent of that impact, we may begin to understand the Southernness of his poetry.

Warren's ambitious poem "Mortmain," which appeared in 1960 in his volume *You, Emperors, and Others,* has as its center the death of the narrator's (presumably Warren's own) father in 1955. The first section of the poem, subtitled "After Night Flight Son Reaches Bedside of Already Unconscious Father, Whose Right Hand Lifts in a Spasmodic Gesture, as Though Trying to Make Contact: 1955," begins this way:

> In Time's concatenation and
> Carnal conventicle, I,
> Arriving, being flung through dark and
> The abstract flight-grid of sky,
> Saw rising from the sweated sheet and
> Ruck of bedclothes ritualistically
> Reordered by the paid hand
> Of mercy—saw rising the hand—
>
> Christ, start again!

In his dying, the father is—predictably but nonetheless powerfully— identified with history, with guilt and debt and also with the human will. In his terror at that apparition, Warren's narrator delivers an absolutely characteristically Warrenesque response: "Christ, start again!" As if starting again were possible here. And yet, paradoxically, it turns out to be, through an unflinching rehearsal of the father's history, and through it, the son's. Mortmain, the dead hand of the past, arrives to exact a debt that cannot be ignored but that can be eventually worked off.

To my mind, what is important about this moment is the impulse to *start again:* not ex nihilo, but in as full cognizance as possible of what has come before: that in fact the essence of starting again, even in moments of profoundest crisis, is an honest and thorough taking stock. The father's unpraised hand becomes emblematic of that demand, that responsibility: "Like law, / The hand rose cold from History / To claw at a star in the black sky." And the narrator of the poem now must take his father— along with the demands of that "law," that "History," that "black sky"— completely into himself.

When I first began years ago to engage Warren's poetry seriously, the one quality that most impressed itself on me was Warren's restless insistence on transforming himself as a poet. In his first books he fully consolidates and masters the Fugitive style; "Bearded Oaks," for instance, is in its way a perfect poem, albeit a relatively minor example of something. Then in 1956—clearly a pivotal year for Warren—the magnificent book *Promises* blasted apart the relative purity of the early work (which in truth had already been seriously disturbed by "The Ballad of Billie Potts"), and from that point forward, Warren never ceased to hammer away at his own poetic assumptions and practices. I want to argue, in fact, that the most completely characteristic fact about Warren's poetry from *Promises* onward is its unwillingness to rest in any achieved style. Warren's poetry *is* a dialectic of change, of internal hammers and tongs and scalpels and sutures and wrecking balls and dynamite all trained inward, challenging its own generating and presiding ethos. Allegiance to what Warren calls "impure poetry" is symptomatic of that transformative restlessness; "Christ, start again" is its battle cry.

But this internal obsession with a sort of mental urban renewal is not simply a stylistic concern, nor does it adhere merely to the practice of poetry. In "The Use of the Past," Warren declares that "the will to change" is the most fundamental of all American characteristics; put simply, he might say that the motto "Christ, start again" could have been emblazoned on the bow of the Mayflower or over the doorway of the First Continental Congress. The selves of individuals, the selves of regions, the selves of nations—phantoms that they are, nowhere to be "discovered" or found, but only flickeringly created—are in Warren's mythos subject to a tortured ancient mariner kind of wandering, and painful and difficult as it is, this condition is necessary and even moral.

We have come to the crux of the argument. So far we have "proved" that the South, like all American regions, is an attitude which is in turn a symptom of a historical amputation, a palpitation in a cultural ghost limb; we have "demonstrated" that a poet, from Warren's perspective at least, is the king of the ghosts, one of those who, importantly but paradoxically, is a purveyor of an infinite regress, the projector of an image of the concept of an ideal; and we have asserted that Warren, as he exists for us in his work, is himself a literary region—which means, given this definition of *region,* that he is a zone containing representative ghosts foreshadowing the existence of other ghosts and is at the same time a patriarch among ghosts, however unhappily so. As such, he might agree with the shade of Achilles in the *Odyssey* that

> I would rather follow the plow as thrall to another
> man, one with no land allotted him and not much to live on,
> than be a king over all the perished dead.

Or would he? Achilles' speech might have an uncomfortable ring in the ear of an attentive and historically conscious white Southerner, particular of Warren's generation. In Southern terms, we know perfectly well who has perforce spent generations "following the plow as thrall of another / man . . . with no land allotted him and not much to live on" and know also perfectly well who has been king over everyone, living and dead alike. Warren himself wrote in 1930 in "The Briar Patch," "Let the negro sit beneath his own vine and fig tree"—a pallid expression of the old separate-but-equal doctrine that would keep African Americans on the farm and "in their place," but at least make the "vine and fig tree" their own.

Christ, start again.

Warren's *Selected Poems, 1923–1975* contains, as one of the new pieces in the opening section of the book, "Can I See Arcturus from Where I Stand," an uncomfortably revealing poem called "Old Nigger on One-Mule Cart Encountered Late at Night When Driving Home From Party in the Back Country." The narrator of this poem, a white man who is driving home late from a party, drunk and distracted by a sexual memory of a woman with whom he has just been dancing, takes a curve too fast and finds himself confronted by the character of the title, discovered in the headlights:

> On the fool-nigger, ass-hole wrong side of
> The road, naturally: And the mule-head
> Thrusts at us, and ablaze in our headlights,
> Outstaring from primal bone-blankness and the arrogant
> Stupidity of skull snatched there
> From darkness and the saurian stew of pre-Time,
> For an instant—the eyes. The eyes,

> They blaze from the incandescent magma
> Of mule-brain. Thus mule-eyes. Then
> Man-eyes, not blazing, white-bulging
> In black face, in black night, and man-mouth
> Wide open, the shape of an *O*, for the scream
> That does not come. Even now,
> That much in my imagination, I see.

The narrator calls the black man and his mule cart a "death-trap," but it is easy to see who constitutes the real danger here: the narrator, one of the profligate kings of the earth, implicitly confident in his ownership of everything and his freedom to do simply anything, is plainly out of control. He goes home and indulges in "the one last drink" and a "sweat-grapple in darkness" with an unidentified partner but wakes again with the image of the mule driver's face in his mind and attempts a poem, which turns out badly.

> And remember
> Now only the couplet of what
> Had aimed to be—Jesus Christ—a sonnet:
> > One of those who gather junk and wire to use
> > For purposes that we cannot peruse.
>
> As I said, Jesus Christ.

In this poem, we can discern one pole of Warren's Southernness: he knows, from the inside, the peculiarly Southern version of racism and can portray its psychology to perfection. He also understands how to project the dangers entailed in the kind of psycho-power the narrator of this poem assumes. It is not merely a reflexive or overfastidious political correctness that leads a careful reader to worry about the profound selfishness the central character of this poem exhibits: he is not only the author of a badly failed sonnet, he is a danger to himself and to others. Warren's poem knows this perfectly well and demonstrates it in another characteristic "Christ, start again" transition:

> Moved on through the years. Am here. Another
> Land, another love. . . .

Between 1930—the year of "The Briar Patch"—and 1956, when he published a strange and fascinating essay called "Segregation: The Inner Conflict in the South," Warren traveled great distances, physically as well as mentally. In "Segregation," Warren travels south as an expatriate, what he calls an "outlander" or a "corrupted native," to talk to Southerners about race relations. Time and space will not here permit a full consideration of this essay and all its ramifications. Suffice it to say that it provides evidence that a powerful "start again," or more than one, had taken place since the complacencies of "The Briar Patch." Interviewing himself at the end of the essay, Warren presents the following Q & A:

Q. Are you for desegregation?
A. *Yes.*

The emphaticness of this *yes* demonstrates that a universe has intervened between 1930 and 1956. The essay "Segregation" is full of contempt for those who evince a "preference for a local and limited point of view," whether conscious or unconscious. Likewise, in the "One-Mule Cart" poem, the narrator who has "moved on through the years," has grown in humanity and understanding. Imaginatively, he revisits the black man, whom he now mentally locates

> By a bare field that yearns pale in starlight, the askew
> Shack. He arrives there. Unhitches the mule.
> Stakes it out. Between cart and shack,
> Pauses to make water, and while
> The soft, plopping sound in deep dust continues, his face
> Is lifted into starlight, calm as prayer.

The poem then concludes with a literal prayer to that image of a concept of a man:

> Brother, Rebuker, my Philosopher past all
> Casuistry, will you be with me when
> I arrive and leave my own cart of junk
> Unfended from the storm of starlight and
> The howl, like wind, of the world's monstrous blessedness,

To enter, by a bare field, a shack unlit?
Entering into that darkness to fumble
My way to a place to lie down, but holding,
I trust, in my hand, a name—
Like a shell, a dry flower, a worn stone, a toy—merely
A hard-won something that may, while Time
Backward unblooms out of time toward peace, utter
Its small, sober, and inestimable
Glow, trophy of truth.

Can I see Arcturus from where I stand?

For all the "improvement" in the thought of the narrator over the un-
divulged distances of the leap at the center of the poem, there are still
deep problems presented by this text's projection of what we have come
in such facile fashion to label "the other." The man at the end of the
poem, after all, is unreal—only a memory construct, arguably a sentimen-
talized one, arguably invoked to aggrandize the narrator, to redeem him.
The real man on the real mule cart remains as unknown and unrepre-
sented as ever. What is most convincing here is the placement of both
characters against a stark and inhuman background—winter night, cold,
the black abyssal starry icy sky. This comes out of the South but is not the
South. It is memory. It is guilt remembered.

I love Warren's work, of course, but in all honesty, I have to say that I
dislike this poem—very likely because I discover in it too many painful
traces of my own experience as a white Southerner. I wish not only that
it had never been written but that the situations and emotions it describes
had never existed or been imagined. Nevertheless, I find it eminently believable. Once racism has raised its cold hand and laid its mortmain on
any mind, it can never be eradicated. No one escapes it; it cannot be es-
caped, it can only be resisted. The most potent resistance this particular
poem presents lies in its Wordsworthian abstracting force. At the end of
the poem the backdrop is no longer an American or even a human region;
it is the vacuum of the night sky, the cosmos, against which our human
profiles dim and flicker, ectoplasmic. Whatever Arcturus may be in fact,
it is not located in Tennessee.

"If," as Warren wrote in "Segregation," "the South is really able to face up to itself and its situation, it may achieve identity, moral identity. Then in a country where moral identity is hard to come by, the South, because it has had to deal concretely with a moral problem, may offer some leadership. And we need any we can get." One implication of this passage is that the South—like other places—has tended to project and promote "immoral" identity, false images of selfhood, false consciousness. The drunk and dangerous narrator of the "One-Mule Cart" poem—a white man who behaves like one of the kings of the universe—is a dramatization of that way of being. What the South—and America, and humanity—ought to claim in Warren is the dire and bitter and sometimes thoroughly unappealing honesty of his struggle. In one of his finest poems, "Homage to Emerson, On Night Flight to New York," Warren's narrator looks out the window of a plane as it approaches landing and thinks,

> I have friends down there, and their lives have strange shapes
> Like eggs spattered on the kitchen floor. Their lives shine
> Like oil-slicks on dark water. I love them, I think.

This is no self-serving projection of otherness; it is an acknowledgment of the utter strangeness of all our lives. Insofar as a region seeks to define itself in a complacency of sameness, it denies the simplest truths about our nature; Warren offers the South the opportunity to claim its own human weirdness. It is an offer we all ought to be eager to accept.

That said, I can also contradict myself by contending that the desire to claim a writer for a region pure and simple seems to me sadly misplaced and also dangerous. More than a waste of time, it represents a failure of imagination. Why would we want to crystallize Warren in the South like a fly in amber? The perilousness of any such attempt lies precisely in the extent to which it denies and falsifies his struggle against his own worst tendencies—the "Christ, start again" for which we ought to value him most of all.

Robert Penn Warren as a Poet of New England

John Burt

"Sunset Walk in Thaw-Time in Vermont" is one of a cluster of poems set in Vermont that includes "Fall Comes in Back-Country Vermont" and "Chain Saw at Dawn in Vermont in Time of Drouth." There are also a number of other poems less closely connected with this central cluster, such as "Vermont Ballad: Change of Season" and other poems from the "A Point North" section of *Rumor Verified*. What these three poems have in common, in addition to the setting and the allusion to the season in all three titles, are common themes, a common outlook on mortality, and a thinly peopled but not totally inhuman imaginative landscape (at least by Warren's standards). Vermont landscapes naturally recur in Warren's poetry, since the Warrens purchased a second home in West Wardsboro, Vermont, and became so attached to the region that Warren ultimately chose to be buried in a rural cemetery not far from there. The Vermont poems define an imaginative and thematic geography different in several ways from that associated with his other repeated landscapes, the story-rich Kentucky and Tennessee border regions of his childhood and youth; the bright but fierce Mediterranean seasides that form the setting for sequences such as "To a Little Girl, One Year Old, in a Ruined Fortress" and "Island of Summer"; the stark clarity of far western landscapes in "Evening Hawk" and "Rattlesnake Country"; the lonely stillness and sadness of the handful of poems set in San Francisco; and the moral confusion and excessive excitement—somewhat heightened by alcohol—he seems to describe in himself in all of his poems set in Louisiana.

Warren's Vermont is one of the least peopled of his landscapes. There *are* people, of course: the nameless passerby in "Change of Season"; the lumberjack who dies a slow but unobtrusive death in "Fall Comes to Back-Country Vermont," with whose passing into anonymity the poet feels an understated kinship; and the nameless other man in "Chain Saw" who hears the same lyric snarl of the saw that the poet hears and who, dying, thinks the same thought that has been bothering the poet, the thought about how little sense life in retrospect seems to make, how little we ever figure out what to do with it. In "Sunset Walk" there is the poet's son, absent to the speaker but present to his imagination, and there is his grandson, unborn at the time of the publication of the poem in 1974, upon whom the poet imagines himself, from the grave, passing a benediction in the loving vigilance of death. None of these, however, are people with the same kinds of pointed and developed stories that persons in the poet's Kentucky have: there is no Slat Gillum, or Dr. Knox, or Big Jim Todd, or Gabriel Penn in the Vermont poems. Even western poems like "Rattlesnake Country" are more populated with individuated characters than the Vermont poems are. Finally, the poet's own character and biography are not foregrounded in the Vermont poems in quite the same way they are, say, in the very painful and personal poems set in Minnesota, such as "Answer to Prayer." The poet's presence in these Vermont poems is chiefly as the Wordsworthian center of lyric perception and not as a biographical individual, although like Wordsworth in "Tintern Abbey" he is still clearly himself and not a generalized person.

What the people of these poems have in common is not a fund of stories or history but a shared sad, accepting reflectiveness about death. In all three poems the speaker has a moment of imaginative intimacy with people who are not in fact present to him (the logger, the patient, the grandson), a moment in which he reflects, with neither fear nor Warren's more characteristic fierceness, on the fragility of human life and the inaccessibility of its meaning. The landscape itself figures in these poems as a place charged with a stern but sober mortality. Mortality in Vermont is very different from mortality in Kentucky (where it is usually attended with a dramatic story) or in the Mediterranean, where its aspect is gritty, edgy, and violent, as for instance in the whole "Island of Summer" sequence.

The title of "Sunset Walk in Thaw-Time in Vermont" introduces the poem as an occasional piece. It seems to arise from the here-and-nowness of a specific occasion. But at the same time, that occasion announces itself in the title as unexceptional. Such titles promise a kind of easy, reflective, low-intensity intimacy with the reader: Wordsworth calls a poem "An Evening Walk" with the implication that it puts one into the immediate presence of the poet's mind as a significant experience unfolds. But that experience, significant as it is, is announced by the title to be but one of many related significant experiences the poet could have chosen. It is *a* walk, not *the* walk; it describes an important point perhaps, but not a turning point. The poem we call "Tintern Abbey" is in fact called "Lines Composed a Few Miles Above Tintern Abbey On Revisiting the Banks of the Wye During a Tour. July 13, 1798." Wordsworth's poem is designed to appear as if it contained just those lines (any lines) the poet *happened* to write, about something that just happened to happen to him at a particular time and place. So "Sunset Walk in Thaw-Time in Vermont" announces itself as recording something that just happened to happen at a particular time of day during a particular season, although Warren is a little less finicky about specifying the particular date and place. Both Warren's title and Wordsworth's are at pains in the same way to understate, perhaps defensively, the importance, indeed the visionary power, of the experience the poems record. The very matter-of-factness of the titles serves to distance both poets at once from the visionary experiences upon which both poems center and from the loss of such experiences, which is their thematic burden.

Such titles promise a peculiar relation to time in that they are intended not to narrate a poet's experiences to a reader but to register experiences as they are in the act of happening and to enable the reader to have kindred experiences in the first person. The poem is the cry of its occasion, and the reader is intended to cry that cry as much as to hear it. Such poems promise an impossible identity in time between the experience the poem relates and the composition of the poem and an equally impossible superposition of the poet's experience *in* the poem and our own experience *of* the poem.

Consider how this relation to time works out in "Tintern Abbey." Both our reading and Wordsworth's composition of the poem require an imaginative leap out of time, for any realistic placing of either experience in time would condemn us both to exactly the kind of inauthenticity, privation, and belatedness the poem expresses fear of. To place his poem in a realistic time, Wordsworth would have to concede his separation from the earlier self with which he seeks in the poem to remain in moral and imaginative communion—not just the lost younger self who saw this landscape five years before, but the equally lost older self who just stood in the same place and wondered, painfully, but at least forthrightly, what had become of him in the meantime. To place the poem in a realistic time would also require us as readers to concede our separation from Wordsworth, a separation that is somehow parallel to the one Wordsworth fears will intervene between his earlier and later selves.

The poem's title speaks from an authentic *now*. But is the date Wordsworth put in his title the date of the experience or the date of the composition? What is the present tense of this poem? Did Wordsworth write this poem while sitting, say, on a stone? Or did he speak it, to Dorothy, and then write it, later, in a present tense that could no longer literally apply? (Or did he, hilariously, write it with Dorothy looking over his shoulder?) Are the thoughts about the meaning and price of experience, the painful comparison of what he is now with what he was five years before, thoughts that he articulated in the poem's very language while having the experiences he describes in the poem? Or is what he had an almost wordless feeling, which he can only articulate into thought while recollecting it in tranquillity?

"Tintern Abbey" and "Sunset Walk" share a vision of what consciousness is, which makes this longing for an authentic present especially painful. If consciousness, as both poems argue, is finally a matter of an inevitable (if sobering and humanizing) loss of authentic immediacy, can any thought about authentic experiences render them without falsifying them? Or does that immediacy flee us always? Both poems insist on locating themselves in an authentic here-and-now, but their subject is the loss of precisely that style of authenticity, and they reflect, from some point after the *now* is over, about what it means that we no longer can win through to such a *now*.

The *now* of "Tintern Abbey's" immediate utterance is a belated one anyway, not the moment of pure presence the poet seems to have had in 1793, but a moment in 1798 after many experiences of self-betrayal and loss. The poet offers—or rather, challenges us to—authentic access to a day in 1798. But on that day he sought, through his imagination, however mixed with feelings of guilt, wistfulness, and wishful thinking, to feel his way back to a day in 1793 in which he was a different and better kind of person. And what he seeks in the poem is finally not restoration of what he once was but reassurance that living has not in the last analysis been a dead loss to him. That is why Wordsworth so often has the air of someone who is trying, without much success, to cheer himself up.

The Wordsworthian experience of a "sense sublime," a shaped duration outside of the ordinary flow of time, transcends the poet's experience of ordinary time (since the real-time experience necessarily takes place on a different scale). The same shaped duration transcends the time of the poem's composition (since real-time composition also takes place on a different time scale from that of a poet's apparently spontaneous utterance—even automatic writing could not be as spontaneous as lyric utterances present themselves to be). And it transcends the time of the poem's reading as well, since what we describe as our experience as readers is not our actual experience of reading (which is often unfocused and sometimes only makes sense in retrospect) but an idealized lyric experience we undergo in an equally idealized reading time, a shaped transformation of our consciousness of the poem as it unfolds in a successive but patterned way in the sensibility. When the poem opens itself to our thoughts and feelings we find ourselves reaching for a timeless presentness that is at the same time extended for a charged but finite and ordered duration within which we grasp the shape and power of the poem as a whole. And within the poems, the speakers reach for a similar presentness in which they apprehend in their lives the same power and wholeness we seek to apprehend in the poem.

Both poems turn on a moment of lyric perception in which the poet steps out of the ordinary flow of time into a kind of intense present in which poet and reader, experience and reflection upon experience, become perfectly transparent to each other. This moment of timeless duration is also fleeting, and the fullness it offers is portrayed in the reflective moments of both poems as already somehow lost despite the imaginative resort we have to them in the poems themselves. And indeed, the loss of the sense of an intense present that at the same time is timeless and has duration, an intense present in which the power and the meaning of one's experiences are subject to an apprehension so perfect that it cannot be articulated without somehow falsifying it, is one of the themes of both poems. Both poems depend upon a shaped experience of inarticulable meaning and of duration beyond time, and both poems also announce the loss of such experiences. Both poems turn on the experience of fallenness and privation by time, yet in both cases a timeless present remains real enough to the imagination that it knows what it is missing and feels the pain of its loss. In both poems the loss of visionary power is itself rendered in a visionary way, although that visionary power is alienated and confronts the poet—even though he is the author of the poem and to that extent the source of its power—from the outside and with a stinging and unanswerable reproach.

"Sunset Walk" opens by superimposing three different shocks. First is the startlement of the partridge cock that the poet inadvertently surprises on the ground. The bird New Englanders call a partridge is actually a ruffed grouse, which Roger Tory Peterson calls a "bird of brushy woodlands, usually not seen until it flushes with a startling whir." That startling whir is of course the first thing we hear: *"Rip, whoosh, wing-whistle."* Our own startledness as readers is parallel with this. The bird's leap is not narrated to us. We experience it directly, in the first person, and, as Calvin Bedient points out, in the present tense, with all of the immediacy of the partridge and with all of the fleetingness of its vanishing. We *run into* these sounds—each with a delicately different meaning, as Bedient notes, and each sound is a repetition of the sound itself as much as a description of a sound, with five stresses, three of them alliterating, in six syllables. The sounds are never put into a main clause, and the explanatory body of the sentence is shunted off into a parallel structure. Even what exactly is making these noises is not identified for another sentence: it is merely an "it" at first.

The narrator is of course as startled as the bird is. Startlement is a species of intense, almost panicked *presentness*. We stare, with the poet, in a moment of suspended here-and-nowness. The moment is timeless, but it is not, however, merely an instant, for it has duration; it is a shaped experience, charged and ordered although out of the flow of everydayness. We are meant to dwell in it in a wide-mouthed state of wild surmise—as if the moment of the poet's experience, the moment of the poet's grasping of the meaning of the experience, the moment of the composition of the poem, and the moment of our reading it were all transparent to each other as a kind of imaginative resort to an *illo tempore*. I would compare this moment to the moment in Keats's sonnet "When I Have Fears That I May Cease to Be" when he stands on the shore of the wide world and thinks, "till love and fame to nothingness do sink." It is a moment of marking time while in a state of imaginative openness to an eternity in which our selfhood is dissolved.

The center of the section is not the instantaneous *now* (actually, three *nows*) of the partridge's flight but the moment of alert stillness that follows it. It is not precisely a moment in which the poet knows something— say, finally understands a proposition he has been wrestling with. It is instead a moment in which the poet becomes knowing, attunes himself to some power to which he can be present, to which he can bear witness, but which he cannot either articulate or master. It confronts him from the outside, and it calls something from within. But what it is is something that demands experience rather than description, and the experience, even as description and narration seek to transform this moment of *being called* into a moment of human wisdom and tender care, is not exhausted by, and is in fact not even captured by, the moral proposition into which it issues: the belief that we are bound to each other by our shared vulnerability and mortality, from which the duty of care and memory descends.

Several things give shape to this experience of mute, awed beholding. The first is the echo of the poet's own surprise as he stands and catches hold of himself—what he calls the "back-flash and shiver of that sharp startlement." Notice the rhythmic energy, by the way, of that line—the juxtaposed stresses of "shárp stártlement," the verbs postponed breathlessly to the ends of sentences, often reached only at the end of an even more breathless or breath-suspending enjambment and emphasized again with yet another juxtaposition of stresses underlined with alliteration:

> In the ensuing
> Silence, abrupt in
> Back-flash and shiver of that sharp startlement, I
> Stand. Stare. In mud-streaked snow,
> My feet are. I,
> Eyes fixed past black spruce boughs on the red west, hear,
> In my chest, as from a dark cave of
> No-Time, the heart
> Beat.

The poet hears something—the beating of the partridge (they do that, to throw you off) and the somehow parallel beating of his own heart, which is a pulse of time out of time, from what, with a kind of inverse Platonism, he calls the dark cave of No-Time. At the same moment the poet sees something—the sunset, which, as Harold Bloom points out, has been up to the moment of the partridge's upspringing hidden by the snow on the black spruce boughs, snow that the partridge knocked off the boughs in the course of its own plunge into the setting sun. The poet stands fixed, transfixed, his almost paralytic stillness emphasized both here and in section 4, in very pointed contrast to the flight of the partridge. The bird plunges into the setting sun. Although in fact the poor thing is merely fleeing for its little life, the language here implies not only self-annihilation but a kind of consummatory leap of faith into death as into a kind of absolute knowledge—the bird "Into the red sun of sunset, plunges. Is / Gone."

Against that sunset the partridge looks black, although if it is a ruffed grouse it is in fact brown. The changing colors of birds against a blazing sky is something of a preoccupation for Warren, and the scene here echoes, with a telling difference, the opening scene of *Audubon: A Vision,* in which the naturalist, with a lover's rapt attention, watches a great white heron, *Ardea occidentalis,* proceed in charged leisure across a sunrise against which its white body looks black.

The difference between that scene and this is not that one is a sunrise and the other a sunset but that Audubon's position in this moment of taut attentiveness is inflected in an opposite direction from the attentiveness here. For one thing, Audubon has been *looking* for this moment or something like it, but it has merely *sprung* upon the speaker here. Audubon is perfectly in control, and the vision he has is one he is perfectly prepared for. And he knows what to make of it. (He knows, for one thing, how the bird really looks, and we hear him thinking that through: "Thought: 'On that sky it is black,' / Thought: 'In my mind it is white.' / Thinking: *'Ardea occidentalis,* heron, the great one.' ") Also, when Audubon's "heart shakes in the tension of the world" he may be in the presence of the same kind of eternity that is shaking the heart of the speaker here, but Audubon has a composure about that experience the poet here lacks. Audubon is not disoriented. What he beholds is the mutual transparency of nature and self, object and imagination, fact and vision. The axis of vision aligns itself with the axis of things (to use Emerson's language), and the outer world, the world of truth, becomes suddenly consonant with the inner world, the world of meaning.

How different is the moment in "Sunset Walk," where this same intense presence of something to be known beyond knowledge seems to leave the speaker lost and homeless. Panic, as Calvin Bedient remarked of this poem, subsides into angst. It is not only that what the narrator sees (the fleeing bird, the sunset) and hears (the beating wings, his beating heart) are emblematic of loss and absence. It is that the presence he beholds here is itself privative. In *Audubon* one presence faces another. But in this poem both inside and outside are empty and not to be mastered. We are not only in the presence of an inner and outer void (a bird-fled landscape, a dark cave of a heart) but also in the presence of a painful doubt about life. In *Audubon* it is clear that at least Audubon himself is reasonably certain what his life means, and in seeking this kind of moment he seeks what Warren said to Peter Stitt was a kind of heroism. But here the speaker is left to wonder whether his life has any meaning. For when he asks "Where have the years gone?" he does not just mean "How did I suddenly find myself to be sixty-nine years old?" but "How is it that I now find myself at the far end of a life that I do not yet feel has even really begun?" The speaker seems to portray his life as something that has passed without his experiencing it. And to experience the authentic *now* of the poem is in some sense to experience not a moment of authenticity but a sense of the impossibility of authentic experience even though it remains so tantalizingly close as to render the alternative stances of alienation and despair unavailable. If the speaker only knew for certain that life had no meaning, he could be happy at least that far. Life does, intensely, have meaning for this speaker, but that meaning will always just barely elude him, will always be just close enough that its distance is painful. (It is the vision of love and separateness Welty had in mind in the passage from her story "A Still Moment" that seems to underlie the passage in *Audubon.*)

The second section of the poem seems to happen on a very different time scale from the first. In real time, the experience described in the first section must take place over no more than a few seconds. The second section requires an active duration of at least several minutes, and in it the poet has imaginative recourse to at least a few hours of actual day-to-day time. The time-suspending but time-shaping experience of the speaker's heartbeat is replaced by the sound of rushing water, not a time-suspending sound, but indeed the headlong sound of time's passage itself. The stream is not only rushing now but has been rushing all day. It has been in the background of the poet's awareness continuously except for those few seconds after the flight of the partridge cock when he hears only his heartbeat.

The stream, swollen with snowmelt, plunges down a small gorge— clearly the one behind the poet's Vermont house. But the motion he describes is not so much the descent of the water foaming down its gorge as it is the lateral weaving and twining of currents and streamlets as the water slithers over itself in the stream bed. This lateral motion is not so much the motion of the *water* as it is the motion of the *stream,* flexing and relaxing in place. Even in the gathering darkness the water glitters in an unearthly way, glinting with a cold, self-generated light as it shifts in the concentration of its own power.

There is a connection between the pulsing water of this section and the pulsing blood of the previous one, but the stream has a cold self-certainty the blood never has. Indeed, the knowledge the water has is precisely the knowledge the speaker rebukes himself for not having in the previous section. The stream "heaves / In the deep certainty of its joy, like / Doom." Now "joy" in Warren always refers to an intense but nonhuman power (even when experienced by human beings), a power attuned to the deep forces that move the world but utterly cold, often quite destructive but at the same time the ground of all meaning. Because it is the ground of meaning, it is also the ground of authentic action, although it is in itself amoral. It is akin to tragic consciousness in Sophocles, or to the Immanent Will in Hardy (who is, not Eliot, Warren's great precursor), or to the patterned but inscrutable power at work in Melville. When Warren describes it, he often invents figures that are the opposite of metaphors. In a metaphor a concrete vehicle conveys an abstract tenor: Doom, we might say, is water. But at heightened moments in his poetry Warren reverses this: water sounds like Doom.

Warren does not in fact see the water in motion in section 2; he only hears it and imagines, accurately, what it must look like. Even this sound—the sound of a kind of absolute being, in which identity is grounded and annihilated at once—is not fully present to him, since he cannot hear the sound of the water clearly, but hears it "slow and numb as upon waking" as he tries to focus the picture in his mind of the water heaving slickly by, moving in the darkness of a world without him, without anybody.

Section three widens the time span of the poem past that day to include memories of a different season. And it includes a different bird—not the startling once-and-for-all partridge, but the comforting daily thrush, always expected at "thrush-hour." There is a different sound here too, not the low-pitched sound of winter water groaning in the gorge, but a lighter sound, the "Shadow-shimmered and deep-glinting liquidity" of a summer stream at a sunset that is beautiful and, unlike this one, not even remotely threatening. This memory seems to be something the poet resorts to as a way of controlling himself, of not being swept away any further by the experience of the earlier two sections. "I have been at home in this scene," he seems to say, "and I will be again." The effect of this is that when he returns to the disturbing present scene he seems to be doing so under his own power: "I am ready" (as it were) "to turn away from the scene I am comfortable with, and I have nerved myself, with as much courage and candor as I can, to face up to the prospect that threatened me."

What follows is a kind of testament, a kind of plea, but it is a very provisional and compromised one. He does not speak from the depth of his being but modestly, from "Whatever depth of being I am," and he asks not to be freed from failure, folly, ignorance, and anguish but to be worthy of it. What exactly is it to be worthy of your failures and folly? Are failure and folly things one has to be worthy of? Are they not things that just happen to one, sometimes because of one's unworthiness?

I think the idea here is that if the speaker is bound to fail and be a fool, since we all are bound to do that anyway, he can at least be true to the form of his failure and have the integrity of following out his own folly rather than anybody else's. Bloom rightly compares this to the failure of Browning's Childe Roland, who in failing in his own way comes to a kind of success—in fact, he does not fail at all, since he does in fact come to the Dark Tower. This kind of failure is a kind of success because it testifies at least to the length of the ambitions that fail: to say that "one's reach must exceed one's grasp, else what's a heaven for," is to say that one must fail because one only has a heaven if one's reach exceeds one's grasp. If one does not fail, it is only because, like Browning's Andrea del Sarto, one's ambitions turned out to be too small. It is better to be made a fool of by a big idea than to be a wise guy about small ones. Even this is a pretty provisional consolation, since it too can so easily turn to a perverse form of extenuation and tail chasing. But provisional as this is, it is a kind of victory, since it testifies to enough self-control to remain in control of his tone, and if he is in control of his tone, then he is not lost to himself, even though whether he is in control of himself may change nothing except whether he is lost to himself or not.

In giving a testament and issuing a plea—to whom, by the way? to God? to nature? to whatever it is out of which he utters poems?—Warren makes the turn, common to this strain of poem since Wordsworth's day, away from a too powerful present into an abstract commitment that is meant to turn that power to account even as it defends the speaker against that power. If I can turn loss into wisdom, even into wisdom only about the inevitability of my own folly, I am at least not totally abject in that loss. I may not have discovered the meaning of my experience, he seems to say, but I have at least refused to be reduced to nothing by it. When Jack Burden of *All the King's Men* proclaims that "History is blind, but Man is not," he means something like this, that even the inevitable historical experiences of self-defeat and folly and failure and loss of integrity can be turned to account by a spirit determined on candor and whatever self-possession candor can provide. Fate, we may say, is meaningless, but the fatal courage it calls forth, while powerless to change it, is nevertheless the condition of what meaning there is. Wordsworth's ability to hear the still, sad music of humanity, likewise, is not taught to him by his apprehension of the beauteous forms of the Wye valley, nor is it even taught to him by the sense sublime through which he sees into the life of things, but only by his sober consciousness of the fleetingness of his insights—it is not what he experienced; it is what his recourse was when he had to do something in order to be not completely made a fool of by the failure of experience.

It would be too much to ask of this request that it postpone darkness. Indeed, darkness not only falls but coagulates on the mountain's east hump, and the new ice crystal that begins to frame its massive geometry in that scene seems to do so in an unspoken rebuke to the poet. The coagulating and freezing is going on "Meanwhile," that is to say, *while* the poet is reciting his testament, as if, which is of course the case, there is nothing listening to which that testament might make the slightest difference. Perhaps the scene is even, pointedly, ignoring him, which would be a further turn of the same screw. But despite all this—and this is the key to the poet's victory, in a way—the language of the end of section 3 is relaxed and accepting, very different in tone from the language used for, not on the face of it, very different events in section 2. The water freezes, and the darkness coagulates, as it were, with the poet's implicit permission, and if permission for what is going to happen anyway makes no difference either about what is going to happen or about our own power, it makes a great deal of difference whether the surrender to the inevitable is done in a self-possessed way or not.

It is this self-possession that makes possible the blessing the poet calls down upon his unborn grandson in the fourth section. Bloom correctly finds the antecedents of this scene in Wordsworth's turn to Dorothy—who, unlike the grandson, has been standing there unbeknownst to us all through the poem—at the end of "Tintern Abbey." This turn to an other is not only a way out of the impasses and narcissism to which a sublime inspiration is subject—it is not only a way of pulling back from what Wordsworth, grasping a tree so as not to be swept away by the unreality of the world, called the "Abyss of Idealism," what Warren elsewhere calls "Pascalian Nausea"—it is also specifically designed to remedy the problem of the alienating sweeping away of time. Wordsworth in "Tintern Abbey" was worried that he was not the same person in 1798 that he was when last he saw that same landscape in 1793. In Dorothy he sees someone on the other side of the painful transition he has undergone—someone who has not yet, but will inevitably, feel the same alienation and homelessness he has, but who will also, he hopes, derive from it the same wisdom and the same sympathy with those who suffer that he hopes he has arrived at. So Warren here sees in his son, and in his imagined grandson, not merely another person whom he can love and to that extent step outside of himself and his predicament, but also someone who will face precisely the same predicament he now faces.

What Warren wishes for the grandson is that he too will stand in that same homeless place, staring red-westward, with the sound of moving water in his ears. But that is not precisely it: he wishes not that the son and the grandson have the same experience of being unable to answer the important questions about life, but that they not be undone by that experience. He wishes, in other words, that they retain the ability to wish, wishing being a kind of having to the extent that it affirms the persistence of the wisher. He blesses them with the ability to bless others with the ability to bless. This paradoxical gift, which perpetually postpones the receiving, is the gift of a kind of self-possession in the face of everything. The son and then the grandson (and so on) are blessed not with the answer to the question "Where have the years gone" nor the certainty that they have been at least worthy of their human failures and folly but with the ability to persist.

At the end of "The Leaf," which concludes the sequence "Island of Summer" in *Incarnations,* Warren had imagined a different sort of blessing, one that moved backward rather than forward through the generations.

The world

Is fruitful, and I, too,
In that I am the father
Of my father's father's father. I,
Of my father, have set the teeth on edge. But
By what grape? I have cried out in the night.

From a further garden, from the shade of another tree,
My father's voice, in the moment when the cicada ceases, has called to me.

The Mediterranean blessing of "The Leaf" is dark and ambiguous, but certainly one cannot miss the edge of cruelty to it. But the Vermont blessing at the end of "Sunset Walk" is its humane opposite.

Warren and the Younger Southern Poets

Interpreting Influence

ERNEST SUAREZ

Literary critics tend to be fond of labels. Allen Ginsberg is a Beat poet; Robert Bly belongs to the Deep Image school; Charles Olson defined the projectivist aesthetic; Sylvia Plath wrote confessional verse; Charles Bernstien is a L-A-N-G-U-A-G-E poet; and so on. By separating contemporary poets into varying movements, critics have put together a version of recent American poetry that not only distinguishes between groups of poets but also traces influences upon certain movements, as well as particular movements' influence upon subsequent poets, in effect establishing literary genealogies.

When a writer does not fit into such narratives, the relationship to his or her contemporaries becomes murkier. In Robert Penn Warren's case there are, of course, histories detailing his connection to the writers of the Southern Renascence. Indeed, Warren has been called a Fugitive, an Agrarian, a modernist, a late modernist, and a New Critic but not a contemporary poet, despite the fact that he won Pulitzer Prizes for poetry in 1958 and in 1979, and despite the fact that there is widespread agreement among those who know his work that his best poetry was written after the mid-1950s. Though there are several good single-author studies of Warren's later verse, there exists no critical narrative situating him within the history of contemporary American poetry. Considering the relationship of Warren's later poetry to the pressures that have helped shape the contemporary poetic canon, as well as reconsidering its relationship to previous Southern poetry, makes it possible to begin to interpret the nature of Warren's influence, particularly on recent Southern poets.

The narratives that currently define contemporary poetic history possess a definite form, beginning with the influence of a modern poet on one or more younger poets who then—as a continuation of or as a rebellion against the older figure's practice—develop an aesthetic that contains certain political associations.[1] For example, Charles Olson sought out Ezra Pound at St. Elizabeth's Hospital in Washington, where Pound mentored Olson, inspiring Olson to turn away from symbolist poetics and toward a creative practice that emphasizes direct treatment of the topical and the local. Olson consequently developed the projectivist aesthetic through the journals *Push* and *Origin* and helped spawn a group of poets—Robert Creeley, Denise Levertov, Ed Dorn and Robert Duncan among them—who studied with Olson at Black Mountain. The projectivist aesthetic, in which the poets' "breath" determines the line, supposedly signals a more natural form of composition, a phenomenon reflected in these poets' rejection of a commercial and artificial mainstream culture. With differing twists and turns, similar narratives are used to describe the development of the other major schools of contemporary American poetry.

One simple reason that Warren does not fit this prototype is his age. Unlike Olson, Ginsberg, Bly, or Adrienne Rich, Warren was already publishing poetry in the 1920s and the 1930s. By the 1950s, when the new schools were developing, Warren was considered a pillar of the literary establishment—someone to rebel against.

Another reason Warren has not fit the model is that he did not seek

1. For examples see Charles Altieri, *Enlarging the Temple: New Directions in American Poetry* (Lewisberg, Pa.: Bucknell University Press, 1979); Steven Gould Axelrod, *Robert Lowell: Life and Art* (Princeton: Princeton University Press, 1978); James E. B. Breslin, *From Modern to Contemporary: American Poetry 1945–1965* (Chicago: University of Chicago Press, 1984); Lynn Keller, *Re-Making It New: Contemporary American Poetry and the Modernist Tradition* (Cambridge, Mass.: Harvard University Press, 1987); Sherman Paul, *Olson's Push: Origin, Black Mountain, and Recent American Poetry* (Baton Rouge: Louisiana State University Press, 1978); Harry Williams, *The Edge Is What I Have: Theodore Roethke and After* (Lewisberg, Pa.: Bucknell University Press, 1978).

followers. He never created manifestos for creative practice or hailed himself as a rebel with a cause, promoting his verse by becoming identified with the political arena. Indeed, Warren was interested acutely in aesthetic matters, as well as in American history and the cultural landscape, but he did not promote his poetry in order to generate poetic schools or to capture the popular political imagination, as, for instance, Bly and Ginsberg with Vietnam, Rich with feminism, or more recently, Carolyn Forche with Nicaragua and El Salvador.

In fact, Warren's most vital influence relates to his lack of interest in billing himself as a "poet with a cause." His influence can be felt most profoundly in his treatment of subject, or in his relationship to ideology, a word that consumes much recent criticism. It is currently fashionable among many academics to say that every work of literature is somehow ideological; even if a work foregrounds the paradoxical and the contradictory, it is viewed as reinforcing the status quo. But this contributes to yet another critical monolith that fails to differentiate adequately between propaganda and thought, a distinction that Lionel Trilling's essay "The Meaning of a Literary Idea" can help put into context.

Trilling distinguishes an "idea" from an "ideology" by claiming that "ideology is not a product of thought; it is the habit or ritual of showing respect for certain formulas to which, for various reasons having to do with emotional safety, we have strong ties." Trilling goes on to hail Faulkner and Hemingway as more substantial writers than Dos Passos, with whom Trilling shared many political sympathies, because of the "activity" with which they tackle "the recalcitrant stuff of life," a quality that provides the "distinct impression that the two novelists are not under any illusion that they have conquered the material upon which they direct their activity."

Warren's later, most influential verse tackles the "recalcitrant stuff of life." Warren presents a poetry of ideas, and of varied conclusions, but not a poetry of answers, not a poetry that closes down on its subject and gives the impression that it has been exhausted. In 1956 Warren stated that authentic poetry resulted from "a tentative spirit, and a kind of—well, I don't know exactly what's the word, except a lack of dogmatism in dealing with your own responses and your own ideas as they come along, a certain kind of freedom and lack of dogmatism under some notion of a shaping process."[2]

This lack of dogmatism distinguishes Warren's poetry not only from much of the work associated with the major contemporary movements but also from much previous Southern poetry, providing an example for younger Southern poets of verse with an emotional and an intellectual range. I would even say that Warren's work avoids an ideological focus largely because at the same time it is and is not "Southern." In contrast, say, to the didactic, often racist and topical "Confederate" poetry and prose of Sidney Lanier, William Gilmore Simms, Thomas Nelson Page, T. S. Stribling, Donald Davidson, Stark Young, and many others, who viewed the South as oppressed by and marginalized from the rest of the country, Warren did not focus his energies on combating external pressures.

In his well-known essay "A Southern Mode of Imagination," Allen Tate details the movement from the "rhetorical mode" to the "dialectical mode" to account for the great leap in quality that Southern literature experienced during the first half of the twentieth century. In a nutshell, Tate states that Southern literature improved because it stopped defending itself from "northern aggression" and became introspective, resulting in the exploration of cultural tensions through the writer's inner conflicts ("the great writer, the spokesman of a culture, carries within himself the fundamental dialectic of that culture: the deeper conflicts of which his contemporaries are perhaps only dimly aware"). Though Tate's claim holds true for Southern fiction, particularly Faulkner's novels, he jumped the gun in regard to Southern poetry. The Fugitive poets, and others whom Tate mentions, are more properly seen as transitional figures. Even much of Ransom's and Tate's best verse—consider "Antique Harvesters" or "Ode to the Confederate Dead"—while not propagandistic, is still shaped by social circumstances that express a strong nostalgia for a previous order. Southern poetry had to wait until the 1950s, when Warren emerged

2. Floyd C. Watkins, John T. Hiers, and Mary Louise Weaks, eds., *Robert Penn Warren Talking* (Athens: University of Georgia Press, 1990), 18.

from a decade-long drought of not completing poems, to find the type of poet that Tate identified.

Like the poetry associated with the major contemporary movements, *Promises* (1957) shows Warren moving away from the modernist emphasis on "impersonality" and toward the more direct and personal. So Warren's later work helped set the stage for a vital contemporary Southern poetry by creating a more personal poetry but, unlike the work associated with the major schools, one that did not close down on the personal or focus on the topical; instead it used the personal to emphasize the fundamental and the universal, a stress that considering the poem "Why Boy Came to Lonely Place" helps clarify:

> Limestone and cedar. Indigo shadow
> On whiteness. The sky is flawlessly blue.
> Only the cicada speaks. No bird. I do not know
> Why I have these miles come. Here is only *I*. Not *You*.
>
> Did I clamber these miles of distance
> Only to quiver now in identity?
> You are yourself only by luck, disaster, or chance,
> And only alone may you believe in your reality.

After establishing the mediative setting, the narrator declares "I do not know / Why I have these miles come. Here is only *I*. Not *You*," emphasizing the distinction between his present self and the self he was as a boy. The question "Did I clamber these miles of distance / Only to quiver now in identity?" is followed by the assertion "You are yourself only by luck, disaster, or chance, / And only alone may you believe in your reality." The change in pronoun—from "I" when the narrator poses the question to "You" when he makes the assertion—indicates the barrier the narrator is confronting. He wants to comprehend something about the shape of his existence, but he cannot even fully connect with the self he used to be. Identity is viewed as a product of "luck, disaster, or chance"—things that are out of an individual's control, so there is no cause/effect pattern that can be shored together so that someone else can understand, not even a "someone else" who is that same person years later. The observation that

"You" can "believe in your reality" only when you are "alone" also reinforces this idea, for neither the boy the narrator once was nor the narrator in the present are alone because, in a sense, they are both there, as the narrator tries to comprehend himself through the self he once was. The word *reality* here means not only one's physical existence but the entire perceptual, subjective, emotional bundle that makes an individual what he or she is at a given moment.

> What drove you forth?—
> Age thirteen, ignorant, lost in the world,
> Canteen now dry and of what worth
> With the cheese sandwich crumbling, and lettuce brown-curled?
>
> Under the ragged shadow of cedar
> You count the years you have been in the world,
> And wonder what heed or
> Care the world would have had of your absence as it whirled
>
> In the iron groove of its circuit space.
> You say the name they gave you. That's all you are.
> You move your fingers down your face,
> And wonder how many years you'll be what you are.
>
> But what is that? To find out you come to this lonely place.

The third stanza begins with an inquiry—"What drove you forth?"—that questions what the boy, "lost in the world" at age thirteen, was seeking by going to that spot. But as we move into the fourth stanza, it becomes evident that the thoughts the narrator attributes to himself as a thirteen-year-old boy are also the thoughts that currently concern him. The language used to describe the world—"as it whirled / In the iron groove of its circuit of space"—stresses the world's indifference to his existence and to his individuality. Indeed, the poem creates a haunting feeling that the narrator's identity has little to do with him, or at least with his volition, a paradox suggested by the thought "You say the name they gave you. That's all you are." The lines "You move your fingers down your face, / And wonder how many years you'll be what you are" are followed by yet another question—"But what is that?"—and the statement

"To find out you come to this lonely place," indicating that the same basic desires that motivated the boy to come to the place still propel the man. While the narrator does realize that he is a different self than he used to be, he does not discover who he is or who he used to be. There is no neat answer. Instead, a significant emotional and intellectual dilemma has been framed in a manner that allows the poem to remain active, even after we finish reading it.

To varying degrees, the most compelling younger Southern poets—David Bottoms, T. R. Hummer, Ellen Bryant Voight, Yusef Komunyakaa, Betty Adcock, Rodney Jones, and others—share this quality. As an example, let me turn to the work of Dave Smith, who has written poetry of a very high order. In the poems "Night Fishing for Blues," "Homage to Edgar Allan Poe," "Elegy in an Abandoned Boatyard," "The Tire Hangs in the Yard," "Colors of Our Age: Pink and Black," "Tide Pools," "The Round House Voices," and others, Smith employs dramatic situations in ways similar to Warren. Like Warren, Smith is often a poet of memory, giving past events form through the poetic process, but again, like Warren, he addresses the personal without tending to exhaust his subject.

Smith most often focuses on coastal and rural Virginia, using these locations as a less abstract mode of entry into fundamental human dilemmas. For instance, in "The Tire Hangs in the Yard," Smith presents a seemingly simple situation—how a narrator's return to a specific location evokes thoughts from different stages of life—to create a troubling meditation on the relationship between time, death, and memory, with the tire serving as a psychological cynosure for gathering violent and turbulent memories that defy rational explanation but that are given an emotional order.

Like "A Tire Hangs in the Yard," Smith's poem "Cuba Night" resembles Warren's "Why Boy Came to Lonely Place," as each presents an individual's attempt to recall the past in order to provide his life with some form. But like Warren's narrator, the man shaving in Smith's poem can only discover more precise ways to frame the questions that preoccupy him:

> The small of the back has its answers
> for all our wrong turns, even the slightest,
> those aches there's no time for, or source,

and the mole in the mirror, a black moon
of sudden importance, can turn your hours
into love's rapt attention. As you shave
an innocent glance into the yard pulls
your lips mulishly—is anything there
more than a choice, a will to live? When

the fly on its back, feet up in dead air
between the storm-double panes, stiffens
it seems a reminder redolent of a word
you can't speak, like history, but feel
as once you felt the shuffle and slap
of your father's feet on heartwood floors.
He would be bathed then, as you are now,
unshirted, coffee starting, his lathered
clownish cheeks white, the dawn oozing red.

Before memories of the narrator's father are provided, Smith establishes larger contexts, indicating his tendency to widen his poems' focus, particularly emotionally. The first two lines—"The small of the back has its answers / for all our wrong turns, even the slightest"—present a narrator uneasy with something he cannot define: "those aches there's no name for, or source." When the narrator thinks of the dead fly—a creature that has been snuffed out for no reason other than the fact that the storm window trapped it—he is reminded of "a word" he "can't speak, like history," suggesting that life's processes—large or small, international or personal—are perhaps incomprehensible. However, a will to understand "mulishly" pulls the narrator toward a question he cannot help but consider. The question—"is anything there / more than a choice, a will to live?"—basically asks if there is a meaning or an order to the world, or is simply existing the sum of existence?

Quizzical, you hear the razor pull closer,
strokes deliberate, hard, almost independent.
Is it death? Only a cafe memory, you two
standing outside, soft night, a radio,
Kennedy declaring over the dirt his one

line only a war could cross. Your mother
wasn't yet meat that a drunk's Ford would
leave in a frogspawn ditch. Then your father
stopped to visit, shy, held your teenage hand,

while along the block many leaned, listening.
Dusk steadily bled all the light from each
face, a voice—maybe Bob Dylan's—said this
is history, and you said what? Same word
when your wife cried I can't stand any more,
whose crying had started under your yes, yes.
You can't smell her stale sheets and no
memory's kiss mushrooms. No late show's
rerun of Bikini atoll keeps flaring at you.

What then? Only azaleas beginning to explode
that must have been planted in that year,
the smudged hand now earth's, with questions
he couldn't answer. His eyes brimmed wetly.
Nobody you know's been to Cuba or cries out
what history means. There's blood on your lip.
The mole has grown. You're starting over,
remembering the floor that seemed to shake
with their love, then with the unslipping of
her nakedness, soap-white. Then the shaving.

The shaving, the razor at the throat if you will, makes the narrator
wonder if death has created this mood. But like the "almost independent"
strokes of the razor, the memories that creep into his consciousness are
seemingly unrelated. Though the poem presents an attempt to make sense
out of past events, in many ways the narrator cannot get beyond a frus-
trating and exasperating "What?" Couched within the memory of Kennedy's response during the Cuban missile crisis is the recollection that his
mother had yet to be killed in a tragic accident, a thing that he could no
more control or understand than "history." Like these thoughts, the memory of his wife crying, "I can't stand any more" brings the "Same word,"
"what?"

The narrator's response to the question—"What then?"—that begins the last stanza suggests how Smith, like Warren, addresses "the recalcitrant stuff of life." The "azaleas" begin to "explode," as the will to live continues, but the "smudged hand" that did the planting also is buried "with questions / he couldn't answer." The line "His eyes brimmed wetly" has no logical connection to what precedes or follows; yet it conveys an emotional connection. The narrator's father's "eyes brimmed wetly" because he could no more answer the questions that trouble his son than his son can. However, like his son, he could feel their poignancy. As the narrator shaves, he remembers his father shaving. He remembers that time is passing ("The mole has grown"), that life contains pain ("There's blood on your lip") and love ("the floor" once "seemed to shake with" his parents' "love"). But he realizes that he possesses no explanation, for "nobody" he knows has "been to Cuba or cries out / What history means." He can only "start over" by continuing to consider those questions that have no answers but must be asked.

Like "Why Boy Came to Lonely Place," "Cuba Night" presents a series of questions. The manner in which each poet addresses those questions provides the basis for constructing a narrative, a genealogy, for contemporary Southern poetry. Of course, not every Southern poet will fit this mold, just as being born in the South does not automatically make one a Southern poet, and certainly not a good one. But starting with Warren, and then Dickey, and continuing to Smith and other recent poets that I have mentioned, there exists a core of related, though by no means identical, poets whose work forms an unaddressed chapter in the history of contemporary American poetry. When Warren's influence on American literature—as a novelist, critic and poet—is assessed in the future, his role as the source for a new Southern poetry may well be viewed as the triumph of his brilliant career.

Medusa, the Movies, and the King's Men

Deborah Wilson

Although Robert Penn Warren's Jack Burden is political side-kick, newspaper man, and historian, he is also a kind of film noir detective figure, a 1940s ironic God/Bogart "brooding on history" and searching for truth throughout *All the King's Men*. Like most film noir investigators, Burden assumes events have a logic that can be traced, an inherent pattern that will emerge from the "gradual piling up of events, then the rush to the conclusion."[1] In his search he must not only sort through all the fathers around him—Ellis Burden, Judge Irwin, and even Willie Stark—he must also find a way to restore and take his place within the patriarchal order such "logic" and "patterns" signify. At the end of the novel, he lives with one father in another father's house while telling the story of yet a third.

What enables this hero's access to the Symbolic Order, what lays the foundation for his ultimate acceptance of the Law (and place) of the Father, is the repression of the feminine, the exclusion of a difference that must be made subject to that Law. As a signifier of lack (castration), the site of radical difference and threat, the feminine represents, in Claire Johnston's words, "the heterogeneity which must form the outside of the Symbolic Order, the excluded that allows the order to exist as an order."[2]

---

1. Robert Penn Warren, *All the King's Men* (1946; reprint, New York: Harvest-Harcourt, 1982), 383–84. Subsequent parenthetical references to page numbers in *All the King's Men* (*AKM*) will be to this edition.

2. Claire Johnston, *"Double Indemnity,"* in *Women in Film Noir*, ed. E. Ann Kaplan (London: BFI, 1980), 105.

Such an ideology, according to David Rodowick, "considers desire to be a fundamental danger to successful socialisation and thus requires the division of sexuality from sociality. . . . Feminine sexuality is always in excess of the social system which seeks to contain it."[3] That excess must be made subject to the Law, must be repressed, contained, and restored to its fixed, "proper" (marginalized) place so that the hero may take his "proper" place at the center of the Symbolic Order.

In typical film noir fashion, the disruption of the order Jack is striving to restore originates in the displacement of the women who form the background for the central male figures acting within a male sphere. Anne Stanton and Sadie Burke, who move outside their culturally fixed roles, can be read as stereotypical film noir characterizations: the good-bad girl (whose true nature constitutes part of the hero's investigation) and the femme fatale/evil woman (who must either be destroyed or redeemed by the hero).[4] And both are contrasted with Lucy Stark, the good woman in the traditional passive victim/wife role. As "displaced" women, Anne and Sadie must be found guilty and punished or else restored as the good object within patriarchy—usually within familial relations, which, as Rodowick points out, "both legitimises and conceals sexuality by restricting it to a social economy defined by marriage—men assume the place of their fathers in the network of authority, and women are mirrored in this network by their relationship to men as wives, mothers, daughters, etc."[5]

Before analyzing *how* that recuperation is performed in Warren's novel, I want to look at the film version, directed by Robert Rossen and released in 1949, at the height of Hollywood's film noir era. Robert Murray Davis' comparison of both versions points out what is inevitable in the

---

3. David N. Rodowick, "Madness, Authority and Ideology: The Domestic Melodrama of the 1950s," in *Home Is Where the Heart Is: Studies in Melodrama and the Woman's Film*, ed. Christine Gledhill (London: BFI, 1987), 272.

4. Christine Gledhill, "*Klute* 1," in Kaplan, *Women in Film Noir*, 14. Gledhill includes this characterization of the heroine in her discussion of these five features of film noir: "1) the investigative structure of the narrative; 2) plot devices such as voice-over or flashback, or frequently both; 3) proliferation of points of view; 4) frequent unstable characterisation of the heroine; 5) an 'expressionist' visual style and emphasis on sexuality in the photographing of women."

5. Rodowick, "Madness," 271.

transition from complex philosophical novel to mainstream movie: "characters, action, and motivation are consistently simplified, even melodramatized, and the political and moral contexts are so severely curtailed that Willie becomes a stock protofascist villain who is to be identified and rejected rather than analyzed and comprehended."[6] A contemporary critic considered the film's portrayal of fascist abuses of democracy "propaganda."[7] And although Warren, who was a consultant on the screen adaptation, praised the film as "a new creation" from the "raw material" of his novel, he added, "The movie, as a matter of fact, does not 'mean' what I think my book meant."[8] I am willing to accept Warren's disclaimer, to a certain extent, because my interest does not lie in whether Rossen's and Warren's versions are equivalent in either meaning or merit. What I do argue here requires a disagreement with Warren, since both the film and novel produce and are products of the same patriarchal ideology that manifests itself in representations of women. Those representations thus embody a more broadly cultural rather than strictly authorial "meaning" and constitute another form of reductive "flattening," or "propaganda," that becomes more visible when film and novel are examined together.

After the title sequence, the first image in the film is of the society page of a newspaper with, at its center, a glamour shot of Anne Stanton and the announcement of her graduation from a school for girls. The image emphasizes her role as social and sexual (although still supposedly "girlishly" virginal), especially when the camera pulls back to reveal Jack's as the gaze we are sharing. Her (latent) sexuality is contained within the frame of the photo and within the "women's section" of the newspaper, as well as through Jack's objectifying gaze. When the editor tells Jack to go cover Stark's campaign, Jack reminds him of a promised vacation and then shows him the picture as the girl who, the boss reminds him, must now wait for him and he for her. Their eventual meeting is filmed as a

6. Robert Murray Davis, "The Whole World . . . Willie Stark: Novel and Film of *All the King's Men*," in *Film and Literature: A Comparative Approach to Adaptation*, ed. Wendell Aycock and Michael Schoenecke (Lubbock: Texas Tech University Press, 1988), 33.

7. Guy Brenton, "Two Adaptations," *Sequence* 12 (1950): 34.

8. Alan Casty, "The Films of Robert Rossen," *Film Quarterly* 20 (1966–67): 9.

traditional romance (they run toward each other, embrace and kiss), and there follows a predictable sequence of the two playing tennis, boating, and dancing, all accompanied by the requisite romantic music.

When the two finally have a serious conversation, Anne expresses her desire for Jack to be or do "something important." Jack's response, "Like your father?"—spoken beneath the prominent and well-lit portrait of her dead father that hangs above them through the entire scene—emphasizes the ultimate aim of the plot: that Jack accept the law and place of the father. Until he is ready for that role, they must continue to "wait," and she remains a good girl. Sexuality is still on hold through Willie's first gubernatorial campaign and through Jack's four years of wandering, during which, at least once, he gazes at yet another glamour shot of Anne in the newspaper—a cue to her unchanged status.

During Jack's early visit to Burden's Landing, Anne and Jack's mother both reveal a stereotypically feminine discomfort with the men's political disagreements, but when Willie Stark finally speaks to a similar gathering a few years later, standing under that same significant portrait of Governor Stanton, Anne is clearly in awe of and attracted to him. She almost totally ignores Jack, and when he and Willie start to leave, she turns her cheek to Jack's kiss while rushing to shake Willie's hand. Later, Jack stands to the side as Anne dances with Willie at a ball, and we watch from Sadie's point of view the revelation of the developing affair. Their "sneaking around" and discussions of divorce, as well as Anne's obvious discomfort, which can be read as shame, indicate that their relationship is sexual.

When Sadie finally tells Jack about the affair, he slaps her in violent response to the discovery that Anne has been transformed from a good girl to, as he stops himself from saying to Anne later, Willie's whore.[9] By

9. There is a surprising amount of physical violence among the main characters in this film. Sadie slaps Jack in an earlier scene in response to a sarcastic comment about Willie's two-timing. Willie slaps Tom in the dressing room for complaining that his headache prevents his playing football. The two are then prevented from a fistfight by the intervention of Jack and Sugar Boy. There are numerous scenes in which men grab and shake women (Jack and Adam both do so to Anne). Although we do not see the scene, Anne tells Jack that Adam hit her when he found out about her affair. Perhaps the most bizarre example

becoming sexual and doing so outside the acceptable boundaries of monogamous marriage, she disrupts the patriarchal order, a transgression that inevitably results (in these plots) in the disruption of the social order as well. In perhaps the major plot change between the novel and film, Anne is responsible for the Judge's death since she, not Jack, tells Willie of the Judge's past crime, information that results in his suicide. It is significant that she is standing between Jack and Willie, shifting her gaze furtively between them, when they hear the shot. When Adam looks up from the Judge's body to see Willie holding Anne's arm, Willie abruptly drops his hand. Moments later, Jack lets Adam know Anne's role in the Judge's death, a role he presents as betrayal, the breaking of a promise.

The film also makes Anne responsible for the deaths of Willie and Adam, since Adam goes looking for Willie upon learning of Anne's affair. In Jack's words, Adam is "an old-fashioned man [who] believes in a sister's honor." When she tells Jack that Willie is going back to Lucy, back to his proper place within the family, the news becomes another way to emphasize Anne's guilt and betrayal, for Jack responds, "At least I walked out on him!" Thus Anne is not the agent of restoration but is instead forced out of her transgressive sexuality by Willie. In the final scene, after Adam and Willie are both dead, Jack "redeems" the good-bad Anne by offering her a proper place and role with him. He argues that they must make the people see Willie through Adam's eyes. Her feminine gaze will not do, since it would indicate agency and subjectivity rather than objectification within the masculine gaze. Their representation of Adam's authoritative vision will thus give meaning to his death. And, more importantly, they will both take their proper places within the family and the restored order.

As I admitted, making Anne responsible for the climactic events in the film is a significant divergence from the novel, yet, even in the novel, Anne still moves from the innocent girl of Jack's youthful romance to Willie's partner in adultery to Jack's lawful wife. Once Adam dies, she

---

occurs when Willie is showing his father the police radio he has bought. The first message they hear reports that a man is "beating his wife again," at which point they laugh, Willie's father in an almost hysterical way.

becomes a ghostly inhabitant of her father's house until her marriage to Jack. She gives her father's house to the Children's Home as "her gift to the ghost of Adam" (438), thereby fulfilling the laws of patrilineage: the house still goes from the father to his son. She has moved from her father's house into Jack's father's house. Although he has a book to write, the only work she seems to have had was the Children's Home—which he now says she "was interested in" (438)—past tense—and she no longer seems to have anything to *do* except *be* the fully recuperated good object.

In fact, all the women in the novel are eventually returned to their "proper" roles within the feminine/domestic sphere. Jack's mother is sent, sans husband (although she leaves her property, her house, to him), to some unknown destination, after proving to Jack that she is worthy of love by revealing that she had loved his father, Judge Irwin. She has, until then, been a blank space, an object of exchange among a series of husbands. Even as she leaves, he describes her face as "a damned expensive present she was making to the world and the world had better appreciate it" (431). In the film, she is merely a weak, almost invisible alcoholic presence, completely dominated by her wealthy husband, whom, she tells Jack, she *has* to live with.

Lucy Stark, always within the role of wife and mother, becomes increasingly static and fixed within that role. At the end of the novel, she has bought into the patriarchy by literally buying the baby she believes to be her grandson and naming the child Willie Stark. On Jack's last visit to her, he identifies her with the house she inhabits: "She was more like the woman the house had reminded me of the first time I had seen it—a respectable, middle-aged woman, in a clean gray gingham dress, with white stockings and black kid shoes" (423). She has been transformed from the "girlish" figure with the Pre-Raphaelite face she was when Jack first met her (59) to an asexual embodiment of the domestic. In a significant plot alteration, the film makes Lucy much older than Willie and sterile (Tom is adopted). She is frequently filmed in the kitchen or serving at the table or on the porch in an apron, and her "schoolmarm" morals are repeatedly juxtaposed with Willie's appetites. For example, at first Willie doesn't drink because she "don't favor drinking," and later his constant drinking becomes a sign of his moral corruption. In fact, she seems, in Sadie's words, "like she's his mammy and gonna blow his nose for him." Even before Willie's adulteries begin, his marriage, the proper place for sexuality, appears asexual.

As Davis points out in his comparison of novel and film, Lucy is "literally neutered" in the film, Jack's mother is "symbolically neutered," and Anne is "made into the flabby heir of Jack's mother"; in fact, "the movie has no fathers and no mothers" and "dispense[s] with the children as well."[10] Davis reads that absence as a representation of the sterility of values, as an indication that the film escapes Rossen's intentions by showing a world that "cannot provide an alternative to Willie."[11] But Sylvia Harvey's discussion of the "absent family of film noir" offers another link between *All the King's Men* and that genre, thus opening another possible reading that includes sexual difference. Although the family is the locus of sanctioned sexuality, it also "conceals sexuality" in the movies of the 40s and 50s, which de-eroticize married couples.[12] Such an emphasis also serves to desexualize woman generally, as a means of repressing feminine desire, and, as Mary Ann Doane argues, "In a patriarchal society, to desexualize the female body is ultimately to deny its very existence."[13]

The figure of Sadie Burke requires just such a drastic erasure. Although the film offers Anne's transgressive sexuality as the primary disruptive force, Sadie is clearly marked as a sexual threat. Unlike the typical femme fatale, she is not beautiful, but her dangerous sexual power is signified within the system of film noir iconography, which uses cigarettes (one of Sadie's perpetual props) as a cue of "dark and immoral sensuality" and, perhaps, "of her 'unnatural' phallic power."[14] Another cue for the femme fatale, the mirror shot, occurs twice in the film. The first is not a true mirror shot, since we see a side view of Sadie but no view of her mirror image. This scene occurs the morning after she has told Willie that he is

10. Davis, "The Whole World," 42.

11. *Ibid.,* 43.

12. Sylvia Harvey, "Woman's Place: The Absent Family of Film Noir," in Kaplan, *Women in Film Noir,* 24.

13. Mary Ann Doane, "The 'Woman's Film': Possession and Address," in Gledhill, *Home Is Where the Heart Is,* 296.

14. Janey Place, "Women in Film Noir," in Kaplan, *Women in Film Noir,* 45.

a "sap" being used to "split the hick vote." In response to his distress, she offers (almost forces on him) the liquor that becomes a sign throughout the film of the corruption that increases alongside his consumption of alcohol. She, then, is marked as the source of that corruption. Sadie's own drinking also signifies her corrupted gender: she is always the only woman drinking with the guys. The sight of her the following morning, putting on lipstick and combing her hair in his hotel bathroom mirror, further marks her, this time as *sexual* corruption. Although they do not seem to have slept together (he is passed out on the bed but still fully clothed), their sexual involvement is clearly foreshadowed here.

The second mirror shot does include both Sadie's face and her mirrored reflection. As she talks to Jack, she looks at Anne's photograph on his dresser and compares it with her own face in the mirror. This is the moment she tells Jack about Anne's affair with Willie, and, as in the earlier scene with Willie, the knowledge she offers is painful. According to Janey Place, the film noir woman's gaze at herself in the mirror is often a sign of "self-absorbed narcissism," of her independence as well as her sexuality, and therefore doubly transgressive, doubly dangerous.[15] The violence of Jack's response—he slaps her—confirms the degree of the threat.

Of course, even without the sexuality, Sadie's independent aggression, her ambition, is in itself sufficient transgression to require erasure. In the novel, her very presence within the masculine/political sphere generates an upheaval in the social order. She gives Stark the knowledge (that he has been a manipulated "sap") that changes his trajectory and the knowledge (through the benefit of her political savvy) that propels him more rapidly on his way; she is the first sexual disruption of his marriage, and it is her knowledge that finally causes his murder. For "normal" relationships to be restored, the patriarchal order must reassert itself against chaos by divesting her of power, an act of recuperation Jack performs in his role as detective, as the figure actually in control of the narrative all along.

Sadie initially gains access to power by participating in the masculine economy: "She had come a long way because she played to win and she didn't mean to win matches and she knew that to win you have to lay your

15. *Ibid.,* 47.

money on the right number. . . . She had been around a long time, talking to men and looking them straight in the eye like a man. . . . [When her eyes] looked at the wheel before it began to move they could see the way the wheel would be after it had ceased to move and saw the little ball on the number" (84). Although she is not playing for matches, neither is she playing for money. On the night of Tom Stark's football injury, Sadie tells Jack that she "could have been rich a long time back" if she had wanted to, and Jack agrees (372). What Sadie wants is the power that she cannot have outside the masculine game. Within their system she "had channels of information closed to the homemaker type" (141), and in this novel "knowledge is power" (312, 313). Jack tells his mother that "information is money," adding that Willie, like Sadie, is not interested in money (126). Instead, Willie is "interested in Willie," using the knowledge he has about people to wield and to keep power.

Whereas Willie uses his power for self-promotion, Sadie must use hers to promote a man to whom she attaches herself. Although she has learned to win at the men's game, the only way she is allowed to play is through a man. She is apparently the one who makes her lover, Sen-Sen Puckett, politically successful, or, as Jack says, she "had put him into political pay dirt" (73) by giving him "the benefit of her gift for laying it on the right number" (85). In spite of being "a very smart cooky" with a great deal of political savvy, Sadie initially works for the Stark headquarters "in some such ambiguous role as secretary" (74). She is sent there to gather information for Sen-Sen as a way to further his career, not her own. Even after she does become a significant part of Willie's campaign, she also becomes his lover, as she had been Sen-Sen's before, thus giving Willie power over her.

Even though Sadie never escapes her subsidiary role, the fact that she is female makes her participation in the men's game a threat to them. Her ambition as well as her sexual aggression are transgressive desires. After blasting Willie about "the Nordic Nymphs" he had two-timed her with, Sadie bursts out of his office "about the way one of the big cats, no doubt, used to bounce out of the hutch at the far end of the arena and head for the Christian martyr" (141). In particularly hostile language that reveals the violence directed against such disruptive women, Jack then describes her face as "a plaster-of-Paris mask of Medusa which some kid has been using as a target for a BB gun"; her eyes are "a twin disaster, . . . a black explosion, . . . a conflagration," all images that allude to the destructive forces unleashed by her transgressive gaze (141). In the scenes that occur after Willie's repeated indiscretions, Sadie's eyes blaze, her hair "lift[s] electrically off her scalp and her hands . . . flay out in a gesture of rending and tearing" (329). Because she is outside the traditionally feminine, she is a castrating monster who turns men to stone, feminizing them by rendering them passive and static in a novel that defines life as motion (150) and in a culture that links mobility with masculinity. Her acquisition of power, even though politically she is still entirely dependent upon a man for that power, is always a threat.

The first time Jack sees Sadie after Willie's death, she has committed herself to the Millett Sanatorium. Now, as she lies on a chaise longue, her Medusa-like face is "a mask flung down on a pillow and the eyes that looked out of it belonged to the mask. . . . There wasn't anything burning there" (408). In a place traditionally associated with women (Elaine Showalter discusses mental illness as "the female malady"), Sadie is powerless and so no longer threatening. Instead, she has become "like a fevered child on a pillow" (410). She is no longer an eroticized body but has been transformed, in Mary Ann Doane's words, from "the site of sexuality into a site of illness," and "the dominance of the bed [becomes] the explicit mark of the displacement/replacement of sexuality by illness."[16] The woman who once wielded power by means of her knowledge, who could be depended upon to keep her mouth shut since she "didn't have any confidant, for she didn't trust anybody" (329), insists that she has not come to this place to "swap secrets" with the psychiatrist (408). But Jack has come there for information, for Sadie to verify what he thinks he knows—that Duffy made the phone call that provoked Adam Stanton to shoot Willie. She is still part of the power structure by means of her knowledge, even though she has physically withdrawn from it, for she knows what Jack does not—that she is the one who told Duffy to make the call.

What finally removes Sadie from the game she has learned to win is the handing over of her secret knowledge to Jack. Her admission of guilt

16. Doane, "The 'Woman's Film,' " 292, 295.

makes her the Medusa that Jack has always seen in her, since she takes responsibility for killing both Willie and Adam. But she justifies herself by claiming that Willie did not live up to his end of their contract; he was going to throw her over for Lucy, in spite of all that Sadie had done for him, after she had "made him" (410). By doing so, he would fix the game so that she would be excluded and powerless. Since the male game is the only one in town, at least in this novel, Sadie decides to withdraw before she is tossed out, but she takes Willie with her. Yet Jack will not give her credit even for the act that proves she has learned the game well. He decides that since her motivation was emotional (traditionally considered a feminine trait), while Duffy's was rational and calculating (traditional masculine attributes), her "act had somehow been wiped out . . . [and] did not exist for [him] anymore" (411). The one woman in the novel who acts is finally denied responsibility for her actions because, even though she plays the game well, she can never be considered a player on her own. She even depends on a man, Duffy, to make the final play for her.

Having rejected Duffy's implied offer to be her new front man, she has no more access to power, and she tells Jack that she came to the sanitorium because it "was the only place [she] could come" (412). There is no other road for her to take, no other direction left for her as a woman. In her letter to Jack, she makes it clear that she no longer cares who knows what she knows. She sends him a notarized statement, making her knowledge a gift to him, since she can no longer participate in the power struggle going on after Willie's death: "You can do anything with it you want for it is yours. I mean this. It is your baby, just like I said" (415). Having given up her last vestige of power, she tells him, "I'll be gone a long way . . . maybe somewhere the climate will be better" (415–16). She does not know her destination. (She gives Jack her cousin's address since she will not have one of her own.) Unlike Anne or Lucy at the end of the novel, Sadie has no husband or child to care for—her only "baby" was the knowledge she has now declared Jack's—and is left to wander aimlessly. Still giving Jack political advice and still concerned about the rules of the game she can no longer play (she does not want him to think she is welching on a deal), Sadie disappears into the unknown.

The Medusa metaphor Jack keeps using to describe Sadie is a clue to her status in the narrative. Teresa de Lauretis compares the mythical Medusa to the Sphinx in the Oedipus story, both monsters who "have survived inscribed in hero narratives, in someone else's story, not their own; so they are figures or markers of positions—places and topoi—through which the hero and his story move to their destination and to accomplish meaning."[17] Once the Sphinx tests Oedipus and qualifies him as hero, she has fulfilled her narrative function: "her question is now subsumed in his; her power, his; her fateful gift of knowledge, soon to be his."[18] Sadie performs that Sphinx-like function with her gift of knowledge and then disappears from the narrative.

But what about her Medusa-like function? Unlike the femmes fatales in film noir, Sadie is no alluring beauty. As de Lauretis points out, "Medusa's power . . . is directly represented in her horribly 'staring eyes,' which are a constant feature of her figurative and literary representations."[19] Whereas Medusa, who was once quite beautiful, is the object of the male gaze (a status Laura Mulvey calls "to-be-looked-at-ness"),[20] she is also a threat to that same gaze, for she has the power to blind, to disrupt, and even to destroy the objectifying process by turning it back upon itself, as Perseus finally turns her gaze back upon her in the mirror of his shield.

Sadie Burke looks men "straight in the eye like a man" (84), and her eyes are constantly ablaze until the scene in the sanitorium, when they no longer seem to belong to her, when there is no longer "anything burning there" (408). Although her eyes flare once in anger during that conversation with Jack, most of the time she averts her gaze, looking out the window or at the ceiling but not at him. In fact, at the moment she admits that she told Tiny to call Adam, the moment she confesses her guilt, Jack stares *at* her until she twice asks him to stop.

Although in his final meeting with her, Jack says, "her eyes had the old flash," she admits that her knowledge "won't stick in law" (412). When

---

17. Teresa De Lauretis, *Alice Doesn't: Feminism, Semiotics, Cinema* (Bloomington: Indiana University Press, 1984), 109.

18. *Ibid.,* 112.

19. *Ibid.,* 110.

20. Laura Mulvey, "Visual Pleasure in Narrative Cinema," in *Issues in Feminist Criticism*, ed. Patricia Erens (Bloomington: Indiana University Press, 1984), 33.

she sends him her notarized statement, he knows it is "no good." Her knowledge, her discourse, is without value in the Symbolic Order. *Jack*, not Sadie, represents the Law of the Father. She is what must be repressed *by* it. Still bothered that Sadie has "seen through" him, has "read [him] like a book," he consoles himself: "At least, I had not had to wait for her to read me. I had read myself to myself" (416). The narrative is, after all, his and not hers; his gaze, his reading of both her and himself, is the "authorized" version.

In the Cass Mastern segment of the novel, the villain is another destructive "spider woman"/femme fatale, Annabelle Trice. According to Jack, "though the journal does not say so, in the events leading up to the 'darkness and trouble,' Cass seems to have been the pursued rather than the pursuer" (164). In his first view of her, Cass compares her to a traditionally acceptable mythological figure, Venus. Verifying her status as the erotic object of a male gaze, he inventories "every feature and proportion" before concluding that "her beauty was her eyes" (165–66). After seducing Cass into an affair that causes her husband's suicide, Annabelle sells her slave Phebe down the river, an act Cass admits is common enough in the world of men, which is vividly proven so by the sale Cass later witnesses in Lexington. When Annabelle mirrors that behavior, she becomes violent and monstrous. In her final meeting with Cass, in language reminiscent of the Medusa-like Sadie Burke, Annabelle's fingers dig deep into the flesh of his arm "like talons" before she rakes her nails down his cheek (178). She speaks with a "wild sibilance" and sobs "a hard dry sob like a man's." His Venus has become unrecognizable to Cass, and he never sees her again. Annabelle's escape from the sexually passive role brings about the destruction of Duncan, Cass, and Phebe, much like Anne's sexual liaison with Willie (along with Sadie's gift of knowledge and power to Duffy) triggers the events that lead to the deaths of Adam and Willie.

The other disruptive, threatening gaze in the novel belongs to the most marginalized woman in the novel, the slave Phebe. Like Sadie's gaze, Phebe's, too, threatens the order that keeps her powerless. When she finds Duncan Trice's wedding ring, she knows that Annabelle's illicit sexuality caused his suicide, and she stares at her mistress with eyes "bright and hard like gold" (175). Annabelle tells Cass, "She knows—and she looks at

me—she will always look at me. . . . I will not abide it!" (176). Her solution is to sell Phebe down the river to some unknown destination, to oblivion, and then give the money to a blind man who cannot replicate that
gaze. The gaze is a position of mastery, and slaves cannot be masters without a revolutionary transformation of power relations. Rather than the
subject of the gaze, Phebe must be its object, a status literalized by the
slave Delphy, whose body Cass sees exhibited to a group of white men in
Lexington. Both Phebe and Delphy must remain objects of the gaze *and*
objects of exchange. These women are subversive threats who appropriate
an "unauthorized" position, and, like Medusa, they are cut off from the
rest of the narrative; *their* stories are not told, and certainly not by them.

As Mary Ann Doane's readings of film frequently demonstrate, "the
woman as subject of the gaze is clearly an impossible sign."[21] And it *is*
impossible, as long as the sons keep replacing the fathers and reading
themselves to themselves—as long as the king's men keep putting the
Symbolic Order, fractured by the feminine, back together again. It is the
subversive critic who must turn a different gaze upon those texts and disrupt their order by making visible what is invisible in them. By *becoming*
the investigator, displacing the authoritative masculine voice-over, the
feminist critic can reveal the monstrous feminine as a constructed illusion,
a trick with distorted mirrors, and can go on to demystify the enigmatic
feminine so that it no longer appears monstrous or in need of repression.
As Hélène Cixous writes, "You only have to look at the Medusa straight
on to see her. And she's not deadly. She's beautiful and she's laughing."[22]
We *can* look her straight in the eye and live.

21. Mary Ann Doane, "Film and the Masquerade: Theorizing the Female Spectator,"
in Erens, *Issues in Feminist Film Criticism*, 51.

22. Hélène Cixous, "The Laugh of the Medusa," in *New French Feminisms: An Anthology*, ed. Elaine Marks and Isabelle de Courtivron (New York: Schocken, 1981), 255.

Gynocritics and the Masculine Writer

Opportunities in Warren Criticism

LUCY FERRISS

Gynocritics, as it was first defined by Elaine Showalter and later elaborated by other feminists, has a very clear political agenda: "to construct a female framework for the analysis of women's literature."[1] Shifting feminists' emphasis from a disparaging analysis of patriarchal texts written by men to "a positive hermeneutic whose aim is the recovery and cultivation of women's culture,"[2] practitioners of gynocritics have thus far focused on reinterpreting hitherto marginalized texts by women with the dual aim of, first, validating their literary concerns in order to include them in the literary canon and, second, exploring their use of language in order to define the communicative strategies by which women express themselves in text. Women's literature, women's culture, women's language. What on earth could such a program have to do with the work of that "manly" writer, Robert Penn Warren?

To reach the answer we must look, first, at the applied rather than the theoretical—because, theoretically, the two arms of the gynocritical approach seem at war not just with patriarchy but with one another. On the one hand, the fact that readers are usually hard put to tell whether any given anonymous piece of writing was created by a man or by a woman

1. Elaine Showalter, *Speaking of Gender* (New York, 1989), 131.
2. Patrocinio P. Schweickart, "Reading Ourselves: Toward a Feminist Theory of Reading," in *Gender and Reading* (Baltimore, 1986), 35.

speaks for canonical inclusion on the principle that historical exclusion has been a matter of sexism rather than literary judgment. On the other, the search for "certain lexical, syntactical, and intonational features characteristic of 'women's language' "[3] speaks for a separate canon defined by gender-determined modes of expression. But if the *theory* of gynocritics is doomed by a culture whose derived notions of "masculinity" and "femininity" have thwarted women authors' conscious or unconscious attempts to express themselves as women, the *practice* of gynocritics has nonetheless opened up stories for which traditional masculinist criticism has had little use. And there is no reason—given, as the "male feminist" critic K. K. Ruthven has observed, that "textual signals of sexuality are rare to the point of being nonexistent"[4]—that a gynocritical approach should not prove equally useful when the author of the text in question happens to be biologically male. A brief look at three of Warren's texts—a novel, a long poem, and a lyric poem—should demonstrate how such an approach affects interpretation.

A model for our shift in perspective might be Elaine Showalter's discussion of Muriel Spark's *The Driver's Seat*, a short novel whose violent plot—a woman deliberately pursues her own assassin—has conventionally been understood as the "neurotic expression of a personal pathology." Showalter effectively demonstrates that through her self-destructive heroine, Spark "has given us the devastated postulates of feminine wisdom: that a woman creates her history by choosing her man [and that] the power to choose one's destroyer is women's only form of self-assertion."[5] Thus the conventional (masculinist) reading, which reduces the main character's motives and action to a psychological defect, is overthrown by the gynocritical reader's shared concerns with the protagonist, who speaks and acts out of a position peculiar to women.

We may fruitfully compare to this sort of analysis the conventional reading of Warren's most famous work, *All the King's Men*. Most judg-

3. K. K. Ruthven, *Feminist Literary Theory: An Introduction* (Cambridge, 1985), 84.

4. *Ibid.*, 111.

5. Elaine Showalter, "Toward a Feminist Poetics," in *The New Feminist Criticism: Essays on Women, Literature, and Theory* (New York, 1985), 134.

ments of the book hold that by failing to find his calling, the book's narrator, Jack Burden, loses the love of Anne Stanton and "hands her over" to the political demagogue Willie Stark, setting in motion the tragic outcome of the plot. In fact, Anne Stanton may also be creating *her* history by choosing her man. We are first introduced to her as "an old maid, or damned near it,"[6] whose relationship with Jack Burden seems based on her being a near-clone of her ambitious brother, Jack's best friend, Adam. Where differences between Adam and Anne exist, they can be traced to differences of gender—the way each swims, for instance, Adam "hard and straight," Anne "curled over forward." The triangle of Anne, Adam, and Jack yields itself to almost any interpretation—homosexual love of Adam for Jack or vice versa, incestuous love between brother and sister, and so on. In a conventional reading of the novel, what matters most is the distinction between what Adam and Anne together represent, that is, a self-motivated altruism that Jack does not have enough sense of self to match. In a gynocritical reading, what matters most is that Jack describes the woman he purports to love almost entirely in terms of her brother, simultaneously binding up her identity with his understanding of who Adam is.

How does this difference in emphasis affect our reading of the book? Both interpretations acknowledge that Adam, to Jack, is a "Success," while Jack is a "Failure." Adam's success is founded not on worldly recognition or wealth but on having "the idea he lived by. . . . To do good" (*AKM*, 236–37), and it is precisely that central idea and altruism that Jack lacks. But whereas conventional criticism, replicating Jack's subordination of Anne's character to her brother's, attributes Anne's rejection of Jack to a diminished version of Adam's idealism, gynocritics looks more closely at Anne as a separate and unified character.

Let us assume, gynocritically, that it is *Jack* (rather than Adam or Anne) who endows the sister with the brother's consciousness. In this scenario, even as rendered in first person by Anne's lover, we find room for some awareness of what actually qualifies Anne's feelings toward Jack

6. Robert Penn Warren, *All the King's Men* (New York, 1946), 40. Hereafter, all page number citations from this novel will be preceded by *AKM*.

when she makes her speech about being willing to live in a cabin and eat red beans with him if he will only *be* someone. Not all women require purpose in their men; some love drifters, and it is easy to imagine a woman naming lack of vocation as a stumbling block when her reluctance is in fact far more complicated. In this case, the complication is not hard to name: Anne cannot love Jack unless he is like Adam. Her reluctance may have much to do with Anne's patriarchal family and little to do with the intrinsic value of leading a so-called manly life. But Jack *himself* needs purpose in his life—it is from that need that he evolves the theory of the Great Twitch—and so he sets Anne up as the demand that cannot be met, thus locating that demand outside rather than inside himself.

Often it has been argued that Jack's lack of purpose in his life is the subtextual theme of *All the King's Men*. But in gynocritical terms, his anomie is less important as a philosophical motif than as a barrier to his obtaining Anne, who is not incidentally objectified by his keen awareness of his own lack. Manifesting both her role as static object and her symbolic purpose is the leitmotif of Anne as an exquisite corpse: "Letting one hand drop to the bed for support, she leaned a little sideways, lifted her feet from the floor, still together, and with a gentle, curling motion, lay back on the white counterpane, then punctiliously straightened out and again folded her hands across her bosom, and closed her eyes" (*AKM*, 295). As the end that must spell Jack's purpose or lack thereof, Anne is the image of death itself, willfully closed off and mute.

On the other hand, of course, Anne does take action in the novel: she sleeps with Willie Stark. The episode, a turning point in the book, does not so much defy internal explanation as render it frivolous. As with the love triangle, any number of psychological reasons for Anne's choice can be put forward—we may as well believe Anne's claim that she loves Willie as Jack's egoistic claim that his moral weakness pushed her toward the Boss. But to the gynocritic, more important than any such speculation is the marginalizing of Anne's impulses toward Willie by the force that must entwine Jack's personality and fate with that of the Boss.

In other words, the *reason* for Anne's affair with Willie is that it propels the plot forward and brings its elements together. Her action directly causes Jack Burden's flight to the West and his subsequent nihilistic theory of the Great Twitch, and it indirectly leads to Adam Stanton's murder of Willie Stark. The deliberate shock value of Anne's episode with Willie, its absence of subjective validity, makes Anne Stanton one of the weakest links in the chain of Warren's greatest novel. Somewhere in the authorial voice that lies behind the I-narrative of Jack Burden, there is a meaningful critique of the self-centered idealism that objectifies Anne Stanton as "something out of the past by which . . . I had been living" and replaces her with "the secret source of all strength and endurance" (*AKM*, 311). Warren is not Jack, and the Jack of the narrative is not Jack the narrator. Nonetheless, on Anne's failure to answer the question of what she is up to, as a subjective character and as a woman, rests the whole problematic nature of narration in a book as reliant on voice as *All the King's Men*. Her *use* is simply too great, too essential in binding together the dramatic plot of the original Willie Stark story and the psychological drama of Jack Burden, to admit of a subjectivity that might destroy the magnificent balance on which the book rests.

That Robert Penn Warren may have had none of this gynocritical exegesis in mind when he wrote *All the King's Men* is, in my view, irrelevant; neither did Muriel Spark have Showalter's notion of the "devastated postulates of feminine wisdom" in mind when she wrote *The Driver's Seat*. The question is, how can a book like *All the King's Men* continue to inform our lives? I have assigned the text to undergraduates in a twentieth-century literature course. They find it dated; they no longer know or care about Huey Long, and the existentialist pose struck by Jack Burden no longer feels natural to them. I have asked students to read the same book in a course on textual constructions of gender, and it has become startlingly relevant—not just in the case of Anne Stanton, but in terms of Lucy Stark, Sadie Burke, and Mrs. Burden, from each of whom Jack flees at one time or another.

Gynocritical approaches to women's poetry have focused primarily on what Alicia Ostriker calls "revisionist mythmaking," the mapping out of new approaches to those myths of Circe, Medusa, Helen, and Rapunzel that underlie Western poetry. Among these myths is the rape of Pasiphäe, the figure inaugurating Warren's dramatic book-length poem *Brother to Dragons*. The fundamental connection between good and evil that such myths commonly illustrate has always been seen as at the heart of *Brother to Dragons*, and it thus provides another example of how gynocritics may abet a renewed study of Warren's work. Like Margaret Atwood's figure of the Siren (who sings "a stupid song / but it works every time") Lucy Jefferson may well come to represent how "the female power to do evil is a direct function of her powerlessness to do anything else."[7]

Lucy Jefferson's voice is the interruptor of the poem's sequence. From the very start, she bursts into healing lyrics of self-castigation, the flip side of which spells rage:

> I loved my children. And love them. But know, too,
> The way my husband's face looked locked in sleep,
> When leaning in the night, the lamp unlit,
> I said, "He lives in some dark place where I
> May come to take his hand, if I love well."
> But never came where he inhabited.
> Came only to Kentucky, by my love.
> I did the best I could. No, that's a lie.
> I did not do my best. I died.[8]

We soon learn that she believes her death was caused by her not doing "the good thing," which would have been to reach out to the horribly beaten George and succor him in the face of her son's wrath (*BD*, 84–85). Lucy's guilt-ridden confessions have sound metaphysical backing, but as physiological or psychological explanations of a possible person's death they are treacle. One's death of natural causes is no evidence of one's failure to do one's best, and moral stasis in the face of obvious injustice—as in the case of the brutalized George—is no prima facie cause for death. Like any post-Freudian mother, Lucy is all too eager to take unto herself

7. Alicia Ostriker, "The Thieves of Language: Women Poets and Revisionist Mythmaking," in Showalter, *The New Feminist Criticism*, 322.

8. Robert Penn Warren, *Brother to Dragons: A Tale in Verse and Voices* (New York, 1953), 22. Hereafter, all page number citations to this work will be preceded by *BD*.

the responsibility for her child's actions—in the hope, if not of seeing her child relieved of responsibility, then at least of having her self-accusations denied by those with more objective views. Instead, she finds her own attempt flung back at her by her brother, Jefferson—"Yes, there's your female fondness back again!" (*BD*, 189)—without ever receiving the absolution for herself that a complete indictment of Lilburne should bring.

Every act in the poem, as R.P.W. observes, "is Janus-faced and double." Lucy, identified by her name as the embodiment of light, is nonetheless a woman and so part of the Earth that clamors, near the beginning of the poem, "Come git it, boy, hit's yourn, but git it deep!" (*BD*, 16). Fleeing the dark, "my dark fear of the dark, and the dark land," she yet sees it as the place where she will be reunited with her husband, who "lives in some dark place where I / May come to take his hand, if I love well." Her son Lilburne, of course, "does not bring the light"—but that rather obvious observation, made by R.P.W., has a less obvious corollary: his failure to bring light is due to the way he "define[s] the human . . . By love of Mother." The intrinsic worth of true mother-love has been confirmed repeatedly by readers of *Brother to Dragons*, but it is not in fact a distinguishing human characteristic, rather one we might be said to share with most mammals. Moreover, the rise in the virtue of loving one's mother suffers from a reductiveness that rings hollow when issues of racial violence are involved. So R.P.W.'s assertion that

> Lilburne had no truck with the Evil One,
> But knew that all he did was done for good,
> For his mother and the sweetness of the heart,
> And that's the instructive fact of history,
> That evil's done for good and in good's name
> (*BD*, 143)

carries a self-pejorative tinge, especially in the smug word "instructive." *Good's name* is not the same as *good*; our refusal to recognize the dark edge to our insistently "light" characterization of the sufficiency of loving Mother in order to qualify as a decent citizen has blinded us more than once to the evil that prevails without regard for such filial sentiment. Hitler adored his mother; Jesus showed little regard for his.

As we have noticed, the responsibility Lucy names for herself is, on the face of it, absurd. Her death was *not* "index of responsibility . . . the infection of my love," but brought on by heart attack; there is *no* evidence that her sons loved her for the "infected nourishment" of fear in her milk, even at the most symbolic level; her fear of the dark is no "crime." Her self-scapegoating does have a more believable subtext, however, named by Charles Lewis when he admits to the "relief" that he felt when his wife died:

> . . . I was no longer
> In need to strive to be worthy of her love:
> Ah, the terrible burden of love!
>
> (*BD*, 97)

As with Jack Burden's reaction to Anne Stanton, Charles' exclamation confuses his wife's love for him with the obligation he feels to love her equally. If there is one distinguishing characteristic of love as agape, it is that it does not lay burdens on the beloved. The love to which Charles refers is—logically enough—eros. If Lilburne Lewis feels that same burden, then Lucy is at least in part right: his insanely sadistic action, done in her name, is caused by lack of agape, of the love that releases its object.

But if we expect Lucy to come to this rounded conclusion, we are disappointed. Unlike the other characters in the dramatic poem, Lucy almost never narrates an event. Instead she picks up figurative threads—her breast milk, the burdens of innocence and guilt, fear of darkness—and continually reweaves them into the cloth of her self-proclaimed responsibility. More than half the time, her speech is interrupted just as she is about to make her point, so that she either fails to finish her thought or alters its emphasis in response to the interruption. Lines like "I begin to see why your rejection of Lilburne" (*BD*, 186) and "What is awful is that I must remember / That all my Lilburne wanted, after all" (*BD*, 189) are never completed. By interjecting her voice into the narrative in its fragmented form, she nullifies the either/or polarity of the poem, the very polarity in which she would have had to participate if she had insisted on completing her lyric uninterrupted. That is, R.P.W. and Jefferson, holding that either evil is total, a thing to be "cast out," or it comes from the desire for good, take her oracular speech as an authoritative vote for the latter. Their own redemption hangs on that interpretation. But the gynocritical reader is not in the same position as R.P.W. and Jefferson. We can see how the narrative drives on toward closure despite the refusal of closure in Lucy's lyric, interrupted speech. And what Lucy has been doing, in large measure, all along, has been questioning the Oedipal plot that lies at the root both of *Brother to Dragons* and, some would say, of masculinist narrative itself.

I am not advocating that we pretend Warren was a woman when he wrote the lines I have cited. Rather, we should make available, for discussion of those issues in Warren with which masculinist criticism has not dealt fully, the open questioning that has been applied, say, to the South African writer Olive Schreiner, who wrote the manifesto *Woman and Labor*. One feminist hears Schreiner's voice as "soft, heavy, continuous, a genuine accent of womanhood, one of the chorus of secret voices speaking out of our bones."[9] Another writes that Schreiner's sense of her status as a white woman is constructed "by way of a racist turn in Darwin's diction"[10] so that the "timeless maternal strengths" she lauds may prove a minute compensation for biological powerlessness. The first of these observations speaks to that undefinable quality "women's language"; the second speaks to the way such language places Schreiner's novels on the cusp of a redefined canon. Dealing, like Schreiner, with race and gender at one blow, Warren may either find himself behind the barricades or in an open field where the so-called gender battle is not so much won or lost as realigned with other factors, including race, class, and historical circumstance.

A shorter poem of Warren's may provide a final guide to new reading. Warren's incandescent poem "The Flower" has been read as a father's

9. Elaine Showalter, *A Literature of Their Own: British Women Novelists from Bronte to Lessing* (Princeton, 1977), 198.

10. Carol L. Barash, "Virile Womanhood: Olive Schreiner's Narratives of a Master Race," in Showalter, *Speaking of Gender*, 271.

love poem to his child—not only a recapitulation of how "all things bent their energies" to a moment between father and daughter, but also a prophesy of future change for the child and the world she will live in. In the general focus on Warren's renewed lyricism in the poems, not much attention has been granted to the expectant stillness of the baby girl in her father's arms as he approaches a field of wild flowers or to her reaction over the flower that she receives.

Flowers themselves, of course, are an easy symbol of initiation into the signs and metaphors of womanhood. The first flower the father gives to the unsuspecting girl—a virginal white bloom—is complemented by the mother's gift of a blue flower, more suited to decorating her hair, whose "yellow" symbolically suggests sexual passion. Stamped with this layered sexual identity, the girl now aggressively asserts her right in the ritual: "You . . . demand your flower" Warren repeats, but in the incident he narrates, the white flower she desires—symbol of feminine innocence—is "by season and sea-salt browned." Though she nonetheless accepts this "ruined" bloom, her parents compensate the loss with a blue flower, and the little girl "sing[s] as though human need / Were not for perfection." Where does the imperfection lie—in the trampled virginity of the white bloom, or in the substitution of the blue flower in gold hair? The images that follow point—rather shockingly, in this context—not to awakening sexuality but to loss of fertility and the dying beauty of "curled leaf and dry pod." The line "Let season and season devise / Their possibilities," which has been understood metaphysically as "a way of transcending time's ruins after the Fall,"[11] thus carries more specific gender connotations: the estrus-linked repetition of "season" in this context suggests both the open future and the closed avenues of the incipient woman's life. For the girl, neither choice—the mess of "deflowered" womanhood or the slow desiccation of the eternal virgin—is perfect. Their alternation echoes in the poem's vividly colored changes toward the end, where a white gull turns black against a blue-gold sky, then in the last light turns white again, finally falling "unruffled" (I detect a female gull here) to the sea.

Read gynocritically—that is, placing the girl/woman's view in the fore-

11. Victor Strandberg, *The Poetic Vision of Robert Penn Warren* (Lexington, 1977), 237.

front of the poem—"The Flower" becomes both ode and elegy. Its narrative and imagery simultaneously prophesy, celebrate, and mourn the choices and sacrifices, some of them determined by cultural constructions of feminine pureness and womanly procreativity, involved in the baby girl's imagined future.

A certain style of literary theory is predicated on the assumption that writing per se, and thus every writer's oeuvre, involves issues of class, race, and gender. I do not issue that caveat. A recent review of William Maxwell's *Complete Stories*, for instance, castigated Maxwell for not writing about racial minorities, poor people, or homosexuals. Like some readers who wrote to the *New York Times Book Review* following that piece, I find the reviewer's mode of judgment itself flawed.[12] But Warren wrote on race directly at several points in his career; and more than one reader has observed that "the most important experience for Warren [is] sexual experience."[13] When these issues are raised in regard to Warren—when portrayals of African Americans in his fiction are questioned or the misogyny of the sex act in *A Place to Come To* brought forward—the knee-jerk reaction has been to deny vehemently that Robert Penn Warren himself was either a racist or a sexist. But this response not only begs the question, it assumes an argument ad hominem that Warren himself would have vigorously discouraged as inimical to discussion of the text. As he said himself of Coleridge, "Even if the poet himself should rise to contradict us, we could reply that the words of the poem speak louder than his actions."[14]

I make this appeal to open the gates, not only toward more aggressive feminist readings of Warren's texts, but also toward readings—we have had some already, particularly in recent work by Randolph Runyon and John Burt—that explore those tricky areas of the poems and novels that

12. The review appeared in *New York Times Book Review*, January 22, 1995, p. 3. Reactions appeared in the *Book Review*, February 19, 1995, p. 39.

13. Arthur Mizener, "The Uncorrupted Consciousness" review of *Flood: A Romance of Our Time*, by Robert Penn Warren, *Sewanee Review* 72 (autumn 1964), 695.

14. Robert Penn Warren, "A Poem of Pure Imagination," in *New and Selected Essays* (New York, 1989), 335. Hereafter, all page number citations will be preceded by *NSE*.

contemporary theory may help us bring to light, not because it is chic to discuss matters of gender, sexual orientation, race, and class, but because the author was dealing with those matters: take Slim Sarrett in *At Heaven's Gate*, for instance, or Frog-Eye in *Flood*. We do him wrong to prefigure his attitudes and subsume them to what we consider the philosophical thrust of the work.

As the narrative theorist Susan Lanser has pointed out, "feminist literary theory is not about gender; it is a thoroughgoing investigation of the premises, goals, and methodologies of the entire discipline of textual studies, and what it hopes to accomplish is a shift in the discipline's paradigms."[15] Or, as the narrative theorist—and he was a narrative theorist—Robert Penn Warren once put it, "We, too, even in our flicker of time, can earn a place in the story . . . by creating the future. That is the promise the past makes to us" (*NSE*, 53). It is fortunate for us that Warren's awareness of history, including the history of the sexes, was profound enough to anticipate Lanser's shift in the paradigm, a shift that could weave his stories into its new cloth. I suspect that he would be less upset than his immediate followers to learn, for instance, that the handful of feminists grappling with his fiction have suggested that we start bringing down the notion of Warren as the one-time genius of *All the King's Men* in order to establish a continuum of involvement with issues of identity and power that invariably include gender.

Finally, seizing some of these dicey issues as opportunities for the next generation of criticism on Warren's legacy, we may find ourselves contributing not only to Warren studies but invaluably to those theoretical discourses that must—however they might deny it—begin with close reading of the original text. Any study of an author like Warren in our time is, as he puts it in *Brother to Dragons*, "Janus-faced and double," looking both toward a fresh approach to a major twentieth-century author and toward the contribution that author can make to our evolving understanding of what constitutes literature. Take the definition of gynocriticism with which I began: "To construct a female framework for the

15. Susan Sniader Lanser, "Shifting the Paradigm: Feminism and Narratology," *Style* 22, no. 1 (spring 1988), 54.

analysis of women's literature,"[16] to emphasize "the recovery and cultivation of women's culture."[17] No one has yet defined exactly what constitutes "women's literature" or "women's culture." We know it is not a literature or culture that excludes men—that would mean works about nuns. We know it has not been fully or solely represented by the writings of women—too many of them have written books that conform to masculinist notions of society and plot, even to the point of representing themselves as male writers. We know it is no longer framed by domesticity, if it ever was. We have begun to recognize, moreover, that "the rich variety of writing by either sex resists any attempt at limiting its nature by sexual characteristics alone."[18] We do best, then, it seems to me, to use the "positive hermeneutic" of gynocritics not only to recover texts by women, but to explore areas where whatever we choose to call female consciousness, including the consciousness of the reader, has affected the world created by a text—whether that world be the invention of a male or female writer, whether its "culture" be populated primarily by men or primarily by women.

Our assumptions about the unity of the literary work are at a far remove from Warren's. Where he sees connections and progression, we are more likely to find seismic faults and fractures. But burnishing those fragments with the grit of language and its relation to the dialectic of society will not tarnish them, but only make them shine the more.

16. Showalter, *Speaking of Gender*, 131.

17. Schweikart, "Reading Ourselves," 35.

18. Peter Schwenger, "The Masculine Mode," in Showalter, *Speaking of Gender*, 101–12.

Robert Penn Warren as Moral Philosopher
A Study in Hope, Love, and Endurance

JAMES A. GRIMSHAW, JR.

Notwithstanding Warren's claims that his work is not a historical novel or that work is not naturalistic or he is not a moral philosopher, his deep and abiding concern over questions metaphysical cannot be denied. His criticism betrays that concern, as may be demonstrated briefly from his essays on Coleridge and Conrad. In section 3 of his masterfully thorough reading of *The Rime of the Ancient Mariner,* Warren addresses Coleridge's philosophical development and view of Original Sin, the "fundamental postulate of the moral history of Man." The Mariner's act of killing the albatross symbolizes man's confrontation with "the mystery of the corruption of the will, the mystery which is the beginning of the 'moral history of Man.'" The criminality of the act appears in three ways, the third of which is "the crime against Nature, a crime against God." Although the Mariner seems to move from love of creatures (sea snakes) to a love of man (key to his redemption), Warren asserts that even in his remorse man is still guilty of "the original crime against the sacramental view of the universe: man is still set over, in pride, against Nature." About Conrad, whom he assessed as a philosophical novelist in the fullest sense of the label, Warren elaborates: "The philosophical novelist, or poet, is one for whom the documentation of the world is constantly striving to rise to the level of generalization about values, for whom the image strives to rise to symbols, for whom images always fall into a dialectical configuration, for whom the urgency of experience, no matter how vividly and strongly experience may enchant, is the urgency to know the meaning of experience." For Conrad and for all writers, composition is a way of knowing.

Evidence from other criticism by Warren could be added. Huck Finn's imagination, Warren notes, is "a way of discovering and dealing with moral fact, a poetry that . . . is concerned with the human condition" and is thus an essential part of Huck's growth. And in the third section, "Moral Assessment," of Warren's introductory poem ("Portrait") to his book on Dreiser, the persona concludes that Dreiser learns "The secret worth / Of all our human worthlessness," a lesson leading from despair to hope, perhaps.[1] In another context, R. W. B. Lewis notes that Warren "has best turned the philosophy and rhetoric of William James to his own masterfully original imaginative ends" in his fiction and poetry.[2] Before turning to a closer look at Warren as moral philosopher, however, two definitions ought to be clarified because the two terms are often indiscriminately used interchangeably.

"*Ethics* (also referred to as moral philosophy) is that study or discipline that concerns itself with judgments of approval and disapproval, judgments as to the rightness or wrongness, goodness or badness, virtue or vice, desirability or wisdom of actions, dispositions, ends, objects, or states of affairs."[3] Louis P. Pojman adds to that definition: *ethics* refers "to the whole domain of morality and moral philosophy, since they have many features in common. For example, they both have to do with values, vir-

---

1. Quotations are from Warren's essays "A Poem of Pure Imagination: An Experiment in Reading," 359–64; " 'The Great Mirage': Conrad and *Nostromo*," 160–61; and "Mark Twain," 116, in *New and Selected Essays* (New York: Random House, 1989); and "Moral Assessment," in *The Collected Poems of Robert Penn Warren,* ed. John Burt (Baton Rouge: Louisiana State University Press, 1998). All citations of Warren's poetry are from this edition, and I gratefully acknowledge Professor Burt's kindness for making an early version available to me.

2. R. W. B. Lewis, *The Jameses: A Family Narrative* (New York: Farrar, Straus and Giroux, 1991), 443. Victor Strandberg also deals with William James's influence on Warren's poetry in *The Poetic Vision of Robert Penn Warren* (Lexington: University Press of Kentucky, 1977).

3. Dagobert D. Runes, ed., *Dictionary of Philosophy* (New York: Philosophical Library, 1960), 98.

tues, and principles and practices, though in different ways."[4] We must acknowledge such definitions at the outset in order to discuss effectively the attention Robert Penn Warren pays to ethical and moral concerns. For the purpose of this discussion, ethical concerns are related to man-made judgments as in the legal system, religious dogma and doctrine, and rules of etiquette; and moral concerns are those virtues/vices that transcend man's definition and that are universal to the human condition. In this context, three virtues that dominate Warren's works are *hope, love,* and *endurance,* the absence of which is often reflected contrapuntally as their respective vices, *despair, apathy,* and *instant gratification.*[5] Based on Pojman's schematic,[6] the foundation moral virtues, such as hope, love, and endurance, are generated from a foundation principle, such as the Judeo-Christian tradition, the manifestation of which is a moral (or immoral) act.

Warren is a writer deeply concerned with moral philosophy, a fact explored by a few scholars on other philosophical levels in relation to his fiction. Harry Modean Campbell saw Warren's imagery in *World Enough and Time* "embodying philosophical commentary which results in abstract instruction." Seven years later in "Philosophy, *World Enough and Time,* and the Art of the Novel," John Rathbun identifies as Warren's dominant themes "the question of man's guilt and sin, his responsibility for history,

4. Louis P. Pojman, *Ethics: Discovering Right and Wrong,* 2d ed. (Belmont, Calif.: Wadsworth, 1995), 2–3.

5. This dramatic device employed frequently by Warren may help clarify Randolph Runyon's warning that "the compendium of philosophic statements [Warren's poetry] quite often appears to make . . . cannot be taken at face value, since they appear in poetic contexts steeped in irony." *The Braided Dream: Robert Penn Warren's Late Poetry* (Lexington: University Press of Kentucky, 1990), 11.

6. Pojman's schematic diagrams the relationship between moral and nonmoral virtues, based on William Frankena's distinction between two types of virtues (*Ethics,* 175):

$$
\begin{array}{l}
\text{The moral act} \\
\quad\uparrow \qquad \nwarrow \text{Enabling virtue (nonmoral)} \\
\text{Specific Rule} \rightarrow \ \nwarrow \text{Specific instance of a value (moral)} \\
\quad\uparrow \qquad\qquad \uparrow \\
\text{Foundation principles} \rightarrow \text{Foundation moral virtues}
\end{array}
$$

his divided self, and his attempts at moral definition of himself." Rathbun notes specifically that "Jeremiah's spiritual journey is from Kantian cleavage between justice and morality to a recognition of the unity of all human activity under the authority of one sovereign moral law." And in dealing with *All the King's Men,* Seymour Gross notes that the novel is " 'about' man's attempt to formulate a moral perspective on the facts of good and evil in a world in which the traditional guides to moral conduct have been obscured by various disruptive forces." More recently, Allen Shepherd has furthered this quest for understanding in his essay "Robert Penn Warren as a Philosophical Novelist." Indeed, as Louis D. Rubin, Jr., has subsequently pointed out, "As a writer of fiction Warren was a philosophical novelist. He defined the genre himself in an essay on Conrad: 'one for whom the documentation of the world [and] the urgency to know the meaning of experience' " are imperative.[7] My point, however, is the focus of such criticism has been, by and large, on Warren's fiction with a few notable exceptions that I shall introduce in the course of this paper.

A sounding of Warren's later poetry in the announced context derives from six rather scattered and seemingly unrelated statements. Warren's interest in ethical concerns may be traced back to his boyhood days in Todd County, Kentucky; but Warren later highlights his concern in an undated letter (*ca.* 1941) to Cleanth Brooks about a radio round-table debate on "Ethical Considerations in Criticism" with Austin Warren, Norman Foerster, Warren himself, and three other faculty, one of whom named Baker challenges *Understanding Poetry* as criticism because that approach "didn't give moral evaluation." When Warren turns the discussion to *Antony and Cleopatra* and states that he thinks Cleopatra is a "good woman," Baker "almost went wild," he tells Brooks.[8] Warren's view is

---

7. Harry Modean Campbell, "Warren as Philosopher in *World Enough and Time,*" *Hopkins Review* 6 (winter 1953): 108; John W. Rathbun, *Modern Fiction Studies* 6 (spring 1960): 47, 49; Seymour L. Gross, "Warren as Moralist," in *Robert Penn Warren's "All the King's Men": A Critical Handbook,* ed. Maurice Beebe and Leslie A. Field (Belmont, Calif.: Wadsworth, 1966), 136; Allen Shepherd, *Western Humanities Review* 24 (spring 1980); and Louis D. Rubin, Jr., *The Mockingbird in the Gum Tree: A Literary Gallimaufry* (Baton Rouge: Louisiana State University Press, 1991), 140.

8. James A. Grimshaw, Jr., ed., *Cleanth Brooks and Robert Penn Warren: A Literary Correspondence* (Columbia: University of Missouri Press, 1998), 50.

teleological and focuses on Cleopatra's actions at the end of the play, actions from which he derives the notion of a "good" person. Almost twenty years later and probably without knowledge of Warren's letter, James Ruoff boldly asserts that "In Warren's teleology only God is King, and we are all of us 'all the king's men.' "[9]

In an interview with Benjamin DeMott in 1977, twenty years after Ruoff's assertion, Warren stated that poetry and novels start "from an observed fact of life and then the search begins for the *issue*—the ethical or dramatic issue—in the fact."[10] That the issue may involve self, knowledge, history, loss, or the numerous other "thematic" concerns identified by diverse literary critics does not preclude the involvement of the foundation moral virtues of hope, love, and endurance. A similar triad is found throughout the Apostle Paul's letters: "So faith, hope, love abide, these three; but the greatest of these is love" (1 Cor. 13:13). Herbert G. May and Bruce M. Metzger, the editors of the New Oxford Annotated Bible, gloss that verse thus: "*Love is greatest* because it is God's love poured into our hearts; *faith* and *hope* are one response to what God has first done." Paul A. Hamar's commentary adds that "Love stands above faith and hope, both of which are essential in the plan and work of salvation [redemption]. . . . Love is the fruition of faith's [could we say endurance's?] efforts and hope's anticipations."[11] And as Northrop Frye observes in *The Great*

9. James Ruoff, "Humpty Dumpty and *All the King's Men*: A Note on Robert Penn Warren's Teleology," in *Robert Penn Warren's "All the King's Men": A Critical Handbook,* ed. Maurice Beebe and Leslie A. Field (Belmont, Calif.: Wadsworth, 1966), 141.

10. "Talk with Robert Penn Warren," in *Talking with Robert Penn Warren,* ed. Floyd C. Watkins, John T. Hiers, and Mary Louise Weaks (Athens: University of Georgia Press, 1990), 228. Louis P. Pojman notes more specifically that the virtue-based ethical systems, "sometimes called *aretaic* (from the Greek *arete,* which we translate as 'excellence' or 'virtue'), . . . center in the heart of the agent—in the character and dispositions of persons." *Ethical Theory* (Belmont, Calif.: Wadsworth, 1989), 289. The emphasis in virtue-based ethics is on *being.* Warren focuses on such agents in both his poetry and fiction. Allen Tate's observation of T. S. Eliot, who was an obvious influence on Warren, that the first stanza of the first poem in *Ash Wednesday* "presents objectively the poet *as he thinks himself for the moment to be*" is germane. "T. S. Eliot's *Ash Wednesday,*" in *Essays of Four Decades* (New York: William Morrow & Co., 1970), 468.

11. *The New Oxford Annotated Bible,* RSV (New York: Oxford University Press, 1973), 1392; Paul A. Hamar, in Stanley H. Horton, ed., *The New Testament Study Bible: Romans–Corinthians* (Springfield, Mo.: Complete Bible Library, 1989), 433.

Code: The Bible and Literature, "The sense in Christianity of a faith beyond reason, which must continue to affirm even after reason gives up, is closely connected with the linguistic fact that many of the central doctrines of traditional Christianity can be grammatically expressed only in the form of metaphor."[12] In explaining the "Poet of Youth" metaphor in *Altitudes and Extensions,* Victor Strandberg treats such themes as a fall from innocence. That "search for the *issue,*" as Warren referred to it, seems to return repeatedly to the doctrine of Original Sin and to culminate in the virtues of hope, love, and endurance—though "obscured by various disruptive forces,"[13] as we have already noted in his analysis of *The Rime of the Ancient Mariner.*

Warren's protagonists in his ten novels lack one or more of those three virtues, and their epiphany, their redemption, relies on the reversal of corresponding vice to virtue, especially the recognition of the potency of love. For example, in *Night Rider* Percy Munn tells Lucille Christian, with whom he is having an affair, that "Love, it's not anything, . . . not when it's not a part of something else"[14] after she informs him that she is leaving. Munn has acted out of selfishness and in vanity, failing to understand and to love himself and, therefore, not understanding and loving others, especially May (his wife), Lucille Christian, and Bunk Trevelyan's wife. Willie Stark, Warren's best-known protagonist and perhaps his most enigmatic character, ironically learns that lesson at the expense of his life at the hands of a jealous mistress (Sadie Burke), a corrupt, ambitious politician (Tiny Duffy), and an enraged brother (Adam Stanton). The working out of Willie's struggle with love is more explicitly recounted in the

12. Northrop Frye, *The Great Code: The Bible and Literature* (New York: Harcourt Brace Jovanovich, 1982), 55.

13. Victor Strandberg, "Poet of Youth: Robert Penn Warren at Eighty," in *"Time's Glory": Original Essays on Robert Penn Warren,* ed. James A. Grimshaw, Jr. (Conway: University of Central Arkansas Press, 1986), 94. James H. Justus notes: "In [the poem] 'Original Sin' Warren gives psychological validity to that abstract necessity, drawn from a full array of philosophical positions and theological doctrines, by commonplace images which accrete rather than develop." *The Achievement of Robert Penn Warren* (Baton Rouge: Louisiana State University Press, 1981), 54.

14. Robert Penn Warren, *Night Rider* (1939; reprint, Nashville: J. S. Sanders & Co., 1992), 440.

stage versions of the Willie Stark story, *Proud Flesh* and *Willie Stark: His Rise and Fall.*[15] And as a third example, in *A Place to Come To* Jed Tewksbury, who himself is a philosophically oriented literary scholar, can finally begin to accept his past when he painstakingly learns that every man must live his own life without recompense for knowing its meaning, finds peace with his past, and seeks reconciliation with his estranged wife, Dauphine Finkel, with whom he had earlier shared a "dark hungering" for truth.[16]

In an introduction to the dramatic version of *Ballad of a Sweet Dream of Peace: A Charade for Easter,* prepared around 1970, Warren acknowledges the grotesqueness of the piece and its origin as a poem and as a summarizing commentary and thematic focus on the earlier poems in *Promises: Poems, 1954–1956,* poems that "turned out to represent a backward-looking reassessment of life and values." The essence of the grotesque is its shock value "to pierce the veil of familiarity, to stab us up from the drowse of the accustomed, to make us aware of the perilous paradoxicality of life." It is emotion-charged attention.[17] In that dramatic version all three virtues or their opposing vices are prevalent. Warren's philosophical concern pervades not only his fiction and drama but also the poetry, to which we now turn in more detail.

Warren's poetry may be conveniently categorized in three phases: the early poems, 1921–1943; the middle poems, 1953–1975; and the late poems, 1976–1989. While his continuing concern with the three foundation virtues carries over between fiction and poetry throughout these years, the following selections from his last volume of poetry, *Altitudes and Extensions, 1980–1984* in *New and Selected Poems, 1923–1985,* illustrate Warren's continuing interest in those virtues. In triadic division, poems

15. Both previously unpublished plays have been edited by James A. Grimshaw, Jr., and James A. Perkins (*Robert Penn Warren's "All the King's Men": Three Stage Versions* [Athens: University of Georgia Press, forthcoming]).

16. Jed Tewksbury, *A Place to Come To* (New York: Random House, 1977), 303, 287.

17. Robert Penn Warren, "The Dramatic Version of *Ballad of a Sweet Dream of Peace: A Charade for Easter,*" in *The Grotesque in Art and Literature: Theological Reflections,* ed. James Luther Adams and Wilson Yates (Grand Rapids, Mich.: William B. Eerdmans, 1997), 245–46.

from sections I–III relate to hope (despair); IV–VI, love (apathy); and VII–IX, endurance (instant gratification).[18]

Sections I and II begin with despair, the absence of hope, and build to a view of hope. Section III contains one long poem, "New Dawn," in which the act performed with great expectations becomes an aftermath of despair. In the lead poem, "Three Darknesses," the "observed fact of life" may be stated in the following current "pop" summary of life: you're born, things happen, you die. The first darkness is the "darkness of wisdom," the realm that the bear and the persona in his "idiot childhood" cannot enter; the second darkness is like Conrad's heart of darkness, with the barrier of communication preventing the persona from learning the mysteries of Black Snake River, of life (could it be for the host "the horror, the horror"?); and the third darkness is the persona's realization of his mortality as he watches an "old-fashioned western" on the hospital TV set. He thinks in a moment of hope, "You are sure that virtue will triumph" and "God / Loves the world"; the hope tarnishes with his concluding thought, "For what it [the world] is." A related thought in his discussion of "The Ballad of Billie Potts" is John Burt's observation: "That one must at once honor and back away from the origin of value is not only the moral conclusion of a typical Warren work; it is also its aesthetic method."[19] Perhaps, however, Warren's issue here is similar to the issue Cleanth Brooks ascribes to Faulkner: "Man is capable of evil, and this means that goodness has to be achieved by struggle and discipline and effort,"[20] *i.e.,* things happen. To carry the point one step further, Jacob Bronowski's observation seems pertinent: "The values by which we are to survive are not rules for just and unjust conduct, but are those super illuminations in whose light justice and injustice, good and evil, means

---

18. Randolph Runyon has presented other interesting evidence for the interconnectedness of Warren's late poetry in *The Braided Dream.*

19. John Burt, *Robert Penn Warren and American Idealism* (New Haven: Yale University Press, 1988), 84.

20. Cleanth Brooks, *The Hidden God: Studies in Hemingway, Faulkner, Yeats, Eliot, and Warren* (New Haven: Yale University Press, 1963), 43.

and ends are seen in fearful sharpness of outline."[21] The persona grasps precisely that "fearful sharpness of outline" of God—unforgiving, cynical, yet loving and wise. Although the "dress rehearsal" of death in "Three Darknesses," part three, causes more despair than hope, the persona in the poem "Far West Once" reflects on his "last tramp up the shadowy gorge" and after sleep "to wake in dark with some strange / Hearthope, undefinable, verging to tears / Of happiness and the soul's calm." Whether his faith is attributable to God or to Nature (are they really separate?) is subject for further discussion in relation to ethical naturalism.

The poem "Rumor at Twilight" opens section II of *Altitudes and Extensions,* and the rumor we learn is the rumor of death, "Like the enemy fleet below the horizon, in / Its radio blackout, unobserved." The "you" of the poem seems to have realized his expectations—financial security, respectful children, a kind wife, perhaps even fond memories; however, whatever significance he has seized and squeezed out of life diminishes in relation to his short-lived place in the universe, which remains unfathomable.[22] That gloomy mystery turns to exultation of the moment as the aged "you" of the poem "Snowfall" stands "in the darkness of whiteness / Which is the perfection of Being," a testimony perhaps magnified by Warren's statement: "Every soul is valuable in God's sight, and the story of every soul is the story of its self-definition for good or evil, salvation or damnation."[23]

Section III contains a very powerful poem, "New Dawn," about the Bombing of Hiroshima.[24] The poem embraces both the hope of success

21. Jacob Bronowski, *Science and Human Values,* rev. ed. (New York: Harper & Row, 1963), 73.

22. I have addressed in more detail this poem, "Rumor at Twilight," in "Brooks and Warren: A Literary Correspondence," at the Center for Robert Penn Warren Studies Third Annual Symposium, Western Kentucky University, Bowling Green, Ky., 22 April 1990. The third poem in section II of *Altitudes and Extensions* is entitled "Hope" and clearly reinforces Warren's concern with this foundation moral virtue.

23. Gross, "Warren as Moralist," 133–34.

24. John Hersey wrote *Hiroshima* (New York: Alfred A. Knopf, 1946), "the story of six human beings who lived through the greatest single man-made disaster in history" (front flap). Warren's poem is dedicated to Hersey and to Jacob Lawrence.

by the crew of the *Enola Gay* and by those behind their mysterious cargo and the despair of Colonel Tibbets, commander, after the mission:

> Some men, no doubt, will, before sleep, consider
> One thought: I am alone. But some,
> In the mercy of God, or booze, do not
>
> Long stare at the dark ceiling.

The middle sections (IV, V, and VI) of *Altitudes and Extensions* shift to the virtue of love, or the failure of love. Burt speaks of Warren's concern with the failure of love: "The danger of love is not only that it is qualified by hatred . . . but that it is in itself a form of exploitation and overmastering of others."[25] However, the vice (antithesis) of *love* in this discussion is *apathy* rather than hate, the antonym of love and an expression of extreme dislike. Apathy is the absence of feeling or the lack of emotion and embodies a crueler reaction more typical of modern Western culture. This substitution does not dismiss Warren's use of hatred as a vice in some of his characters. In *Jefferson Davis Gets His Citizenship Back*, Warren's narrator, in his fumbling at recollection and trying to immerse himself in the "dark flow" of that historical moment, thinks: "We have more, and more words now, and being truly adult is largely the effort to make the lying words stand for the old living truth. How often we learn in later life, for instance, that the love we long ago thought we had was a mask for hatred, or hatred a mask for love."[26]

The poem "The Distance Between: Picnic of Old Friends" (IV) portrays the absence of love in a sexual encounter that left "infinite / The distance between them"—the old friends, now "lovers" (my term). The value of love is replaced by a quest for self-knowledge in "Muted Music" (VI); the "you" in a hayloft wonders "if that empty, lonely, / And muted music was all the past was, after all." The absence of love in the "you" may reflect what Bronowski has claimed: "the values which we accept

25. Burt, *Warren and American Idealism,* 66.

26. Robert Penn Warren, *Jefferson Davis Gets His Citizenship Back* (Lexington: University Press of Kentucky, 1980), 24–25.

today as permanent and often as self-evident have grown out of the Renaissance and the Scientific Revolution. The arts and the sciences have changed the values of the Middle Ages; and this change has been an enrichment, moving towards what makes us more deeply human."[27] For the persona may learn "the only sound that truth can make." Similarly, in the poem "Winter Wheat: Oklahoma" (VI), the old farmer returns from the field to an empty house, "Now no smoke in the chimney," and ruminates:

> But who
> Could be sure about God taking care of His business? Wheat in,
> And maybe He'd go skylarkin' off this time,
> Like He does sometimes to pleasure Himself,
> Whatever He does. And lets
>
> A man's honest sweat just go for nothing.

Though love is lost, in the poem "If Snakes Were Blue" (VI) hope remains a possible fulfillment: "In the distance lift peaks / Of glittering white above the wrath-torn land."

In Warrenesque counterpoint, however, "Last Walk of Season" (IV), "Old-Time Childhood in Kentucky" (V), and "Last Meeting" (V) extol in their individual, quiet ways the meaning of love. Rather than despair, the couple in "Last Walk of Season" is

> thinking of happiness. In such case,
> We must not count years. For happiness has no measurable pace.
> Scarcely in consciousness, a hand finds, on stone, a hand.

Or, in "Old-Time Childhood in Kentucky," the grandfather reduces the basis of happiness to such simplistic truth. "Grandpa," the grandson asks,

> "what do you do, things being like this?" "All you can,"
> He said, looking off through treetops, skyward. "Love
> Your wife, love your get, keep your word, and
> If need arises die for what men die for. There aren't
> Many choices.
> And remember that truth doesn't always live in the number of voices."

27. Bronowski, *Science and Human Values,* 51.

The poem "Last Meeting" touches on "The Negro virtues which," Brooks notes, "Faulkner praises in 'The Bear'[:] ... endurance, patience, honesty, courage, and the love of children—white or black."[28] The persona encounters after forty years his "black mammy," now a "shrunken old woman / With bleary eyes and yellow-gray skin, / And walking now with the help of a stick." Though too busy to see her again, he is touched by her nurturing love, her endurance: "But I'm hangen on," she declares, "fer what I'm wuth."

Hope, love, endurance. These virtues make up the triad in Warren's moral philosophical concerns. In addition to the standard definition of *endurance, i.e.,* duration, the word also means "the capability of acting with moral courage and strength" (*Webster's Third New International Dictionary*). In the first context, Runyon's point is well taken: "Any sustained reading of Warren will at some point have to concern itself with his lifelong meditation on the nature of time," by which endurance is measured.[29] In the second context, Brooks's illustration of Faulkner's characteristic drama of moral choice in "An Odor of Verbena"—that is, Bayard's resolve not to kill again[30]—compares nicely to "Prime Leaf" and Thomas' obedience to his father's suggestion that he turn himself in, a certain death, based on what a man *ought to do.* In his poignant reminiscence of his father, Robert Franklin Warren, Warren recalls his father's words: "The first thing a man should do is to learn to deny himself," proclaiming in their own way the single quality of self-control that seemed to underlie everything for his father.[31] The contrast is the instant gratification that characterizes modern Western culture and usually *a*moral, if not *im*moral, acts.

The two poems "Youthful Picnic Long Ago: Sad Ballad on Box" (VII) and "Sunset" (VIII) reflect a kind of instant gratification. In the first poem

28. Brooks, *The Hidden God,* 42.
29. Runyon, *The Braided Dream,* 8.
30. Brooks, *The Hidden God,* 30–34.
31. Robert Penn Warren, *Portrait of a Father* (Lexington: University Press of Kentucky, 1988), 71.

the moment is the melancholy mood manipulated by the guitar player at the campfire as the persona wonders, years later, whether

> But even back then perhaps we knew
> That the dancing fingers enacted
> A truth far past the pain declared
> By that voice that somehow made pain sweet.

It is purely speculation because at that moment hearts were young. In contrast, the persona in the poem "Sunset" is older and more experienced, as the thought he contemplates indicates: "Oh, what shall I call my soul in a dire hour?" The demand for knowing *now* invokes no act of moral courage. In fact, one might wonder whether it is, as Burt claims about another character, Willie Stark, "moral recoil against moral language which underlies his argument that expedience, and nothing more, is the source of value."[32] The poem's persona explains further:

> The dire hour
> Is the time when you must speak
> To your naked self—never
> Before seen, nor known.

If the persona has his way, he will not wait for that hour.

Endurance manifests itself in the next two selections, "Last Night Train" (VII) and "Milton: A Sonnet" (VIII). The "hundred and eighty pounds of / Flesh, black, female, middle-aged" on the commuter train from New York—that woman whose snore "Is suddenly snatched into eternity" by the departing train—puts the persona in a reflective mood of a lost past, the "uncountable years beyond" his own "little aura of pale-green light"; and he feels "Like blessing the unconscious wallow of flesh-heap / And white sandals unstrapped at bulging of instep." Again through metaphor, readers might recall the Faulknerian character Dilsey and Faulkner's emphatic belief that man will prevail.[33] In the sonnet,

---

32. Burt, *Warren and American Idealism,* 145.

33. See William Faulkner, "Address upon Receiving the Nobel Prize for Literature," in *The Portable Faulkner,* rev. ed., ed. Malcolm Cowley (New York: Viking Press, 1967), 724.

Warren praises Milton's moral courage in the face of a disruptive force—blindness—to overcome "burgeoning Space" and Time in order to "leap like a gleaming fish from water into / Sunlight." But combining this virtue and its vice in Hopkinsesque meter is the last poem in *Altitudes and Extensions,* "Myth of Mountain Sunrise" (IX). The myth, "the old tale told," endures like the stone-incised words "against disaster of granite" and records the instant gratification of "The sun [blaze] over the peak," a repetitious gratification in metaphor. Thus will Nature endure in words as well as in physical appearance, notwithstanding man's folly, perhaps.

Philosophical issues, among them hope, love, and endurance, are also expressed implicitly through image and metaphor in Warren's book *Portrait of a Father,* which includes the earlier poem sequence, "Mortmain." In a 1970 interview with Ruth Fisher, Warren stated: "I don't think of a philosophy as a finished product. Certainly not for a man like me. It's a way of thinking about your life as you live."[34] More specifically, then, readers might conclude that moral philosophy provides a mirror for Warren's poetic thoughts about life; it also provides another way for readers to relate to Warren's writing and, thus, to his legacy.

34. "A Conversation with Robert Penn Warren," in *Talking with Robert Penn Warren,* 187.

Warren's Ventriloquist
J. J. Audubon

DAVE SMITH

James Weldon Johnson is said to have written his autobiography in five separate versions, a comic idea which, upon reflection, will startle few writers. *Who are you?* life asks the writing man. Robert Penn Warren's poetry, as intensely as any major contemporary poet's, grapples with this question. His answers are shifting, multiple, contingent upon circumstance. He said in *Fugitives' Return*[1] that the greatness of an art lay in its ability to create and hold the single image of a man. He knew a life is a history, a narrative, a journey for which the final redemption of meaning seldom if ever comes convincingly to the traveler. Yet he believed in poetry's redemptive life-telling that confronts fate, and he celebrated that in his strangely blended and iconic poem *Audubon: A Vision*,[2] a poem of lyric voice performing narrative tasks.

Audubon: A Vision seems a curious, aberrational poem however it is approached. In her review of the book, Helen Vendler, a most reluctant admirer of Warren's, called it an elegy and a parable.[3] Others have called it a narrative and a history in verse. *Audubon* purports to chronicle the life of the American naturalist, artist, and entrepreneur John James Audubon, who lived from 1785 to 1851, the act of a biography. The poem is

---

1. Robert Penn Warren, *Fugitives' Return* (Vanderbilt University Press, 1959), 143.
2. Robert Penn Warren, *Audubon: A Vision* (Random House, 1969).
3. Helen Vendler, *Part of Nature, Part of Us* (Harvard University Press, 1980), 88.

spoken by an omniscient but hardly indifferent narrator. Its final moment, however, is given undeniably to, and is abruptly spoken by, the poet Robert Penn Warren who almost defiantly assumes an autobiographical post. If *Audubon*'s pedigree seems an odd intercourse of the pastoral elegy and the frontier tall tale, the book is perhaps circumscribed only by recognizing it is an autobiography disguised as a biography disguised as a narrative legend disguised as a narrative poem, all serving to forge the image of a man and a language in which he can exist.

What drew Warren to such an infolded, layered work? His early verse was indebted to the authorial effacement of modernists T. S. Eliot and Thomas Hardy who, in 1928, published his last book, *Winter Words*. Then a Rhodes scholar at Oxford, Warren had been writing poems with John Crowe Ransom since 1921 and, as Allen Tate's roommate at Vanderbilt, he gleefully illustrated "The Waste Land" on their dormitory wall. Modernist that he was, he did not easily accept himself as subject or speaker of his poems. There is no overt autobiography that might have offered us, as James Olney says in *Metaphors of Self*, "the symptomatic key to all that he did and, naturally, to all that he was."[4] He refused the self-explaining statements such as poets are apt to make about the writing of poems—Poe's "Philosophy of Composition," for example, or fastidious Tate's "Narcissus as Narcissus." Yet Warren's first book, published in 1929, was a life study, *John Brown: The Making of A Martyr*,[5] and life study would be Warren's interest, whatever the genre he favored, over a remarkable seventy years of writing.

Unlike Hardy, who wrote his own biography and published it in his second wife's name, Warren often stated vigorous opposition to seeing his life rendered into biography. Yet he cooperated with Joseph Blotner, whose *Robert Penn Warren* appeared in 1996.[6] This "life" has, regrettably, too little of Warren's life in it. I am tempted to say that all we have, truly, of an indisputable Warren life is the collected interviews, *Robert Penn*

4. James Olney, *Metaphors of Self* (Princeton University Press, 1972), 4.

5. Robert Penn Warren, *John Brown: The Making of A Martyr* (Payson and Clarke, 1929).

6. Joseph Blotner, *Robert Penn Warren* (Random House, 1996).

Warren Talking,[7] but any Warren poem, a "talking," is an autobiography of a speculative, alert, self-measuring consciousness in an enigmatic world. His lives are never merely well-recorded historical events. Each poem is a visitation of a life engaged in a struggle between an interior self and an exterior determinism; the struggle is always to observe a self who possesses and employs knowledge. It would be pretty to say this life was Warren's own. Pretty but perhaps not wholly accurate. The life he offers is neither autobiographical nor biographical, but dialectical and hypothetical, a living in, and of, words that compose a man. *Audubon: A Vision* is Warren's starkest rendering of that story.

James H. Justus tells us, in *The Achievement of Robert Penn Warren*, the problem in Warren is always "an adequate selfhood, a breaking out of the debilitating sense of incompleteness and fragmentation. The price," he says, "for that integration of self is not the loss of certain spiritual certitudes, but their hopeful and sometimes desperate testing."[8] Such testing is, of course, directed at self-repair and self-creation, and a full individuation requires living into consciousness. The Audubon of Warren's poetic biography passes precious little life, and what appears is far more cerebral than physical. No historian or student of Audubon has claimed the man owned the introspection Warren attributes to him in this poem, yet Warren requires, and gives him, a life of both significant deed and knowledge in order to demonstrate the value of humane ideas. Audubon's life, embodying the competing attractions to art's individualistic pursuit and community's self-compromises, and moreover displaying the embryonic struggles at the frontiers of country and imagination, seems in retrospect an ideal vessel for Warren's vitalizing.

It apparently looked otherwise to Warren. Published in 1969, the year I entered the United States Air Force and dead in the middle of the Vietnam War, *Audubon: A Vision* had proved difficult for Warren to write. He had started it in the 1940s, worked desultorily on it, but could not come

7. Floyd C. Watkins and John T. Hiers, Jr., eds., *Robert Penn Warren Talking: Interviews 1950–1978* (Random House, 1980).

8. James H. Justus, *The Achievement of Robert Penn Warren* (Louisiana State University Press, 1981).

to the "frame for it, the narrative line" despite the completed, sealed, and available life shape of the long-dead Audubon. Rumors have indebted Warren to both Eudora Welty and Katherine Anne Porter, who had themselves employed Audubon. Finally, as Warren said, he determined to write the work in "snapshots of Audubon," and he claimed that *Audubon*'s form came to him in a sudden rush while he made up the bed.[9] It is an amusing suggestion of a craft-driven modernist's negotiations with Romantic inspiration.

Warren's narrative preparation and skills were established facts—a "long foreground" as Emerson said of Whitman's first work—well before *Audubon* became a gleam in his fancy. His seventh book, *All the King's Men*,[10] had won the Pulitzer Prize in 1946. His eleventh, *Brother to Dragons*,[11] published in 1953, was a verse tale, much admired for its historical, philosophical, and moral probing of Thomas Jefferson's murdering nephews and juxtaposed to our national conviction of American righteousness. If Warren's form trouble seemed mitigatable by his abilities, Audubon's factual life was openly, indisputably available. The young explorer, Jean Jacques Audubon, bastard son of a French sea captain and his Haitian mistress, had been treated by at least nine full biographies prior to Warren's work. Several were published in the 1960s when Warren's creation simmered, and it seems at least likely Warren would have read them. Audubon's *Ornithological Journals*,[12] long in print and reissued in 1967, would have given Warren as much self-perceived character and as many dramatic life events, boldly embroidered if not invented, as a novelist might require. If Warren had ten Audubons to choose from, why was there a form problem? In fact, searching for a narrative line may have deflected Warren from recognizing that was not his difficulty at all. The trouble was a voice appropriately modulated.

9. Watkins and Hiers, 235.

10. Robert Penn Warren, *All the King's Men* (Harcourt, Brace, 1946).

11. Robert Penn Warren, *Brother to Dragons: A Tale in Verse and Voices* (Random House, 1953). Revised by the author as *Brother to Dragons: A Tale in Verse and Voices: A New Version* (Random House, 1979; reprint, Louisiana State University Press, 1996).

12. Maria Audubon, *Audubon and His Journals*, vol. 2 (Charles Scribner's Sons, 1897; reprint, Dover Editions, 1994).

Predictably terse, Warren's comments on the making of the poem imply he lacked not so much a formed knowledge of Audubon as a feel for the inner man. The poem moved rapidly forward when, as Warren said, he began to see Audubon as "a man who has finally learned to accept his fate. The poem is about a man and his fate." Warren, at the time of publication, was sixty-four, with two children roughly the age of those America had watched the Chicago police bludgeon the year before at the Democratic National Convention. Many of us recall how those years produced moments of decision, suddenly made, upon which entire lives seemed later to have followed. Warren's form problem apparently diminished as he came to feel drawn closer to Audubon's inner life.

Warren's attraction to Audubon's life story reaches deep into the sources of identity, beginning with a sense of a Kentucky connection in both lives. Beyond that, Warren's passion to live and work by the imagination and his feeling for the artist as both exile and frontiersman made Audubon a powerfully attractive ancestral model only two generations behind him. Audubon must have looked to Warren like the exemplary American success story as it ought to be, rather than as it so often became—a tale of consumptive and exploitative greed that makes heroes of Gatsbys.

The point of Warren's original interest in Audubon will probably never be known, but we can be sure of an awareness by the mid-1930s. Always compelled by history's actors, Warren, during his tenure at Louisiana State University in the late thirties, could hardly have been ignorant of Audubon. Lewis P. Simpson, in an essay that describes Warren's residences in Baton Rouge, observes that Warren so enjoyed driving his car, even over then primitive roads, that he did not hesitate to purchase property twenty miles out from the university, commuting to his academic duties.[13] Only slightly farther to the northwest was the river village of St. Francisville, where Audubon had lived and painted the portrait of Miss Elizabeth Pirrie in the fall of 1821. Long synonymous with America's nature world, in Louisiana Audubon is virtually the emblem of an ancestry

13. Lewis P. Simpson, "Robert Penn Warren and the South," *Southern Review* 26, no. 1 (winter 1990).

that is itself identified with raw vitality of creature and place. Bird prints, elaborately framed survivors of his great portfolios, grace living rooms, law offices, and dental parlors. Zoos, schools, and roads bear Audubon's name. Audubon, the old man, must have seemed to Warren, in 1936, as immediate as did that new man, Huey "the Kingfish" Long, and Audubon's effort to live as an artist must have been especially telling to Depression-era eyes.

When Warren left Louisiana for Minnesota in the fall of 1941, he remarked that no place would ever look the same—indicting both the rank frontierism of poverty politics and the relatively unchanged beauty Audubon had known. It might be hard for a man to make a life of art anywhere, but Audubon had done it in swamps and in circumstances lived daily in Louisiana. Warren knew Audubon was far from ordinary. He was, nevertheless, a come-here immigrant who landed in the east, lighted out for the west, and though no genius, developed a talent for representational art. He also had the ability to organize people and resources to realize his talent's potential. Who was ever more American than Audubon, the entrepreneur marrying art and business? He spent desperate years, but in the end, as Hollywood would script it, Audubon triumphed. He wanted and got it all: his girl, Lucy, children, money, fame. He proved wrong the ubiquitous doubters and naysayers, the privileged and the established, becoming even before Poe our favorite icon, the rebel whose cause was a driving passion for an art turned to a vocation, a vocation that amounted to a virtual autobiography of the New World man wrestling out an appropriate relation with determinist Nature. Before Audubon's portfolios, paintings of birds seemed cataloged, lifeless abstracts. Audubon put birds into life scenes, made them realistic and dramatic and with background contexts gave them a life story. Discovering species theretofore unknown, he expanded the New World's American language with art and made it one whose consciousness remains and lives.

In *Robert Penn Warren and the American Imagination*, one of Warren's best readers, Hugh Ruppersberg, admires "the dialectic of idealism and pragmatism" that *Audubon* pursues. But, fuzzily to my mind, he says Audubon "seeks to lose himself" in frontier wilds:

He desires merger with nature, the loss of self, transcendence to an identity larger than his own—nature's. He learns in the forest that such a merger is unattainable: he inhabits the real world, of which the wilderness is a part. His thwarted desire for merger transmutes into a desire to preserve the wilderness of his vision in artistic form. Art becomes his means of merger, of transcendence.[14]

I am inclined to think Ruppersberg merely trapped in hyperbole until he remarks, "It is the ideal which matters." Not the life aspiring to a gritty balance of ideal and actual? Where in Warren is the ideal so privileged, the same ideal that, like the zealot of good cause, becomes so often our worst enemy? Audubon does not want to be lost, to transcend anything, or to merge with anything—unless of course his passion for painting represents that merger. If so, it is odd that the poem unequivocally minimalizes practice of the art. Audubon's painting is mentioned only twice in the poem. This Audubon does not draw or paint; he watches, and we watch him *watching*. Or he scouts, hunts, conducts business, and is said to learn to define himself against the world. "The world declares itself," Warren writes. Audubon can declare nothing until he has a language of integrated being, a real self. The evidence of that self may be the painting, but we see little of it. Or it may be the growth of consciousness, and there is a deal of talk about that. How else is Warren to give this Ulysses an uncounterfeitable signature? How retrieve from the deadness of time and his own actual life story an Audubon whose speech lives to redeem us, a form problem indeed?

Warren's solution was, at any rate, under his nose and it was imagistic, if not cinematic. He recognized in Audubon's bird portraits the artist's manipulation of foreground and background, the paradox of time and distance, bountiful wildness and rapacious civilization. He saw how Audubon contrived the illusion of life's movement to survive and even to flourish in the most natural contingency and circumstance. Audubon had painted birds from corpses he killed, putting them in realistic contrast to

14. Hugh Ruppersburg, *Robert Penn Warren and the American Imagination* (University of Georgia Press, 1990), 79–80.

symbolic landscapes, a procedure that served as an opportunity to reveal Audubon's growth of consciousness. Warren knew, as Joseph Conrad had written, that art's intention must be to "render the highest kind of justice to the visible universe." And, snapshot to snapshot, each idiosyncratic in length and subject, Warren caused a figure of Audubon to stand still, to watch, then leaped him years ahead by exposition, image bridges, even quoted passages from Audubon's journals, always emphasizing helplessness of phenomena before determinist fate. But Warren had also learned from Conrad that for the greatest artist "justice to the visible universe" is not enough. That artist is "one for whom the documentation of the world is constantly striving to rise to the level of generalization about values, for whom the image strives to rise to symbol, for whom images always fall into a dialectical configuration."[15]

Because Warren's problem was the tale of the inner man, he needed a strategy to draw out the dialectical configuration he knew Audubon's life story carried. Typically, poems of the life story begin and end somewhere, survey events and occupy a large stage of time, providing context that manifests struggle sufficient for a life's redemption of historical anonymity. *The Divine Comedy*, *The Prelude*, *Song of Myself*, Ted Hughes's *Crow*, and Bishop's *Geography III*, however diverse in strategical imperatives, remain life-story dramas. Warren once chastised John Greenleaf Whittier for failing to submit his poems to life tests, for an "unconditional surrender" to pure emotion, which meant Whittier and his poems did not know life fully enough. What Audubon knew, and it was adequate, had been described in a scene in the *Ornithological Journals* called "The Prairie." Maria Audubon's edition of the journals notes that the incident occurred in the spring of 1812, in the upper midwest plains, when Audubon was thirty-seven years old.[16]

Warren transposes this scene to "The Dream He Never Knew the End Of," section II of the book's seven parts. At 197 lines, the section represents nearly half of *Audubon*. Its domination of the whole is such that no other event in Audubon's life is given in anything more than shorthand

15. Robert Penn Warren, *Selected Essays* (Random House, 1951), 58.
16. Audubon, 230.

exposition. Although Audubon said his journals were "food for the idle," they reveal him to have been a man of discipline, one greatly busied by a career to which he was utterly devoted, roving over the American frontier as few did, or could, obviously delighting in abundant experiences of every sort. Why, then, did Warren choose to represent his life in a single anecdote portraying Audubon as, at the least, accessory to murder?

The answer may lie in recognition of responsibility that a man assumes for the life he walks in. To Warren, the quest for language is always a self-definition. Warren's poem begins in rhetoric with definitions of Audubon. Part I locates young Audubon mythically, historically, and chronologically by lies attached to his name and origin, by describing his passion for the woods and its mysteries, by his lack of language. Audubon remains a stiff and standoffish character, however, where definitions, distancing and controlled as they are, revealing as they do Audubon's recognition of "How thin is the membrane between himself and the world," fail to make an Audubon "self" knowable. Part II, therefore, cuts to Audubon in action, seeking a night's shelter at a cabin he has come upon in the woods. Admitted by its resident hag, he feels himself direly threatened by her and her two crude sons. Guilty of uncivil, inhospitable, and ugly behavior, but not of actual assault, mother and sons are hung to death, and left hanging, by Audubon and three conveniently arrived quasi regulators:

> The affair was not tidy: bough low, no drop, with the clients
> Simply hung up, feet not much clear of the ground, but not
> Quite close enough to permit any dancing.
> The affair was not quick: both sons long jerking and farting, but she,
> From the first, without motion, frozen
> In a rage of will, an ecstacy of iron, as though
> This was the dream that, lifelong, she had dreamed toward.

Watching her about to die, the narrator (in a droll pun by Warren) "becomes aware that he is in the manly state." A brilliant anecdote of loneliness, fear, lust, murder, and complicity becomes, because of Warren's gift of consciousness to Audubon, an allegorical window through which a great life story springs. But whose story is it? Audubon's or Warren's?

This narrative of evil and slippery justice telescopes a man's life to a single event about which all else, before or after, must orbit like lesser stars. It prepares for multiple readings, some of which Warren simply does not follow—Audubon's responsibility for three deaths, for example, and the American Adam's hypocrisy. Some are faint soundings—the fairy tale victim of the woods, a creation myth, a Narcissus myth, the artist's individuation legend. What is given conflates the gift of Audubon's biography and impressionistic portraits of the woods world. Except for "The Dream He Never Knew the End Of," Warren abandons narrative structure nearly presumptive for a life story and makes his *Audubon* out of forms of rhetoric and lyric essentially in the manner of a pastoral elegy. He does so to emphasize the dialectic of a man who passes through crisis to control. Warren's problem all along has been to establish and sustain a voice that must carry a life tale without the abjured narrative chronology.

The unusually static structure of *Audubon* chains images to initiate rhythmic movement for that life voice. Warren's snapshots frame, isolate, and project continuity of image and event relationships; they support interpretability. Like panels in a morality play, these variably constructed moments arrange a stage furniture to contextualize an action that is suggested only, not actual. With Audubon we watch a marvelous bear, a bee glade, a perfect blue of skies and ponds; we hear a thrilling tusked boar and the oceanic roar of buffalo. To that extent, we experience a life Audubon measured in his journals as "in all conscience *perhaps* as good as worlds unknown."[17] So genuinely sweet seems this life, as a "walk in the world," that Audubon risks forgetting the rude lesson of the hanging tree. He may imagine life is ever bountiful even as he dreams of Lucy's lips that "gleam in the bright wind," but it is exactly then that he "cannot hear the sound of that wind."

The reader can hear it well enough, however, for the voice of Warren's narrator strategically moves from liquid evocation of beauty to an intense and gravelly register that is naturalism's countervoice. This dual sounding directs us as clearly as Little Red Riding Hood's path. Braiding a pastoral celebration of nature with an abrupt, chopped, sometimes choked lingo

17. Audubon, 230.

of brutal, muscular consonants; of broken syntax; and of phrases sawed off to hover in white space, Warren carves a style that seems as documentary as his snapshots. Refusing the authority of an autobiographical "I," his panel poems yoke objectivity to a management of time and space by line signals and gestures readers of poetry are never quite prepared for, especially readers who expect the silky traditional voices. Warren baits us with a life story we already know, and may envy, only to overwhelm us with the drumming death-wind news all flesh is heir to.

The narrative of a life story assumes a unified pattern, even a metonymic shape that extends empirically backward and forward as it mimics chronology and implies paraphrasable meaning available only in comprehension of the whole. Thus, the narrative shape subordinates lyric, image, and what Warren, after Conrad, called "dialectical configuration." Lyric, conversely, emphasizes the immediate image, here and now, as a carrier of transcendent opportunity. Subordinating narrative to lyric pressurizes art visually. It also invests discrete moments with density and may impart hypertropic significance to a single experience. Warren's life of Audubon does precisely that.

Most of what a man lives, like much of what passes for poetry, is surface, convention, the rounding off and filling in, the fitting into expected form that is interstitial between moments that are everything. Art being long and life short may encourage aberrant symmetry in poetry, but in life's beginning, middle, and end we feel the truest pattern exists. We may not trust the song of happy experience, but we cling to its hope because we have had moments of joy which validate the hope for more. Audubon's boyhood, his lonelinesses, his feelings about paintings, travel, a favorite landscape, even his dreams arrive at a paltry sum, as Warren says: "He died, and was mourned, who had loved the world." What he left behind were the paintings that collectively express "the dream / Of a season past all seasons." According to Warren, the maker/watcher, this was enough. Or it ought to have been enough, for anyone's life story known through the detached perspective of time and space comes to little more. And yet, that little more matters.

Readers of poetry, like readers of life stories, regard all pattern breaking suspiciously. Had Dante abandoned his terza rima at any point, it would have meant a no-confidence gasp from his audience. The establishment of the voice telling the life story carries the essential authenticity of life. Warren wanted that voice to register lyric response to Audubon's fate, but he chose to violate reader expectations of the life-story form, which legitimately might have emphasized greater balladic, metric, grammatic, and aesthetic regularity. The points of violation, or imbalance, are so extensive that they constitute a kind of anti-poem, as the poem is itself a melange of genre strains. If we expect Audubon's long life spread visibly and symmetrically, Warren gives us several days. If we expect unity of time and place, Warren introduces a Northwest Orient airliner passing over the head of a narrator standing in no defined place. If we take Audubon to represent nature's exquisite beauty and permanent succor, Warren's imagery is blunt in denial with a portrait of a sky like "the inflamed distance" where the dawn is "redder than meat." Nowhere is Warren more undermining of expectations than in the most elemental unit of poetry, the line, whose rebellious and confident note is evident from the opening section of the poem. (Line function tends to be mirrored in Warren's stanzaic improprieties.)

Beginning in medias res, his voice catechistical and surging against the left margin, rebounding, noisy with its alliteration, boisterous and yet controlled, if barely so, Warren flares the stage lights upon Audubon:

I. Was Not the Lost Dauphin

Was not the lost dauphin, though handsome was only
Base-born and not even able
To make a decent living, was only
Himself, Jean Jacques, and his passion—what
Is man but his passion?

Saw,
Eastward and over the cypress swamp, the dawn,
Redder than meat, break;
And the large bird,
Long neck outthrust, wings crooked to scull air, moved
In a slow calligraphy, crank, flat, and black against
The color of God's blood spilt, as though
Pulled by a string.

>   Saw,
> It proceed across the inflamed distance.
>
> Moccasins set in hoar frost, eyes fixed on the bird,
> Thought: "On that sky it is black."
> Thought: "In my mind it is white."
> Thinking: "*Ardea occidentalis*, heron, the great one."
>
> Dawn: his heart shook in the tension of the world.
>
> Dawn: and what is your passion?

Each of the first four stanzas comprises a single sentence broken across lines as jagged as rocky ground. Pronouns have been pruned away; sense momentum has been decapitated for felt instability at line's end, sometimes a dizzying interrogation. The sentences twice bark "Saw" and are then immediately tamped by details which are ensconced by commas, forcing the reader to pull forward against line inertia. By the time he has juxtaposed watching Audubon to the great heron, lyric tension winds so tight that what Warren calls "the tension of the world" throbs. The sonic character of an opening in hymn meter so radically differs from Warren's that you can hear the life whoof from the words. Consider this alternative:

> I was not the lost dauphin though
>   handsome was only Base-
> born and not even able,
>   to make a decent living, was
>
> Only myself, Jean Jacques, and my
>   passion—what is man but
> his passion? Saw, eastward, over
>   the cypress swamp, the dawn. . . .

A stanza of colloquial iambics goes no better, I think:

> I wasn't any lost dauphin, handsome,
> just badly born, not able to make a
> decent living, only myself, Jean Jacques
> my passion—what is man but passion? I. . . .

The slackness in both decasyllabics and hymn meter points up the force with which Warren's improvised sound conveys rhythmically the drama of consciousness that is to come. Imagistically, sonically, literally, the first scene stands Audubon outside of nature's kingdom and gives him Adam's task of naming the creatures. The voice is not Audubon's; it is not Warren's. It is the voice of the biographer, hieratic and indisputable, correct for the prologue that sonorously marks this triadic moment with man, creature, and God.

This voice is the composition of an unusual line signature, one Warren has evolved almost entirely after *Promises* (1957),[18] what might, arguably, be called the first of his major collections of poetry. It is especially unusual in establishing an identity in the free-verse idiom, which typically sacrifices line signature for content effect. Any two or three lines by Warren are readily known as his, but is it so for such poets as Milosz, Rich, or Walcott? Line employment and composition in *Audubon* are not radically different from Warren's late work, but lines are pared to a functional minimum that assaults unexpecting readers and in that assault carry the death-wind news of all flesh.

The common reader expects narrative verse presented in a conventional metric of more or less insistent regularity that concludes typically in patterned sound identity, or rhymes. Modern poets first abandoned rhymes and next put aside lines of recurring numbered elements, whether syllables or stress, or both. This has produced dismay among the uninitiated, who mostly do not write such lines. But it has led equally to a weakened conception of what a line is and what its functions may be. The line, generally stated, advances external action, describes scene or circumstance, and in various ways embodies the mind's consciousness. Lines are thus declarative, imagistic, or rhetorical.

The declarative states, informs, accumulates information. It is built ordinarily in standard English word order (subject, verb, complement) and seeks completion in thought or action, tending to make a statement sufficient unto itself, which may be a full or a partial sentence. This line minimalizes connotative suggestion while enhancing narrative or discursive

18. Robert Penn Warren, *Promises: Poems, 1954–1956* (Random House, 1957).

movement and thus may be known as either a dramatic or a rhetorical line.

Where the declarative line tends to completion, the imagistic line tends toward continuity or spillage; hence it displays the resonance of enjambment. Indeed the "poise" of a line in the grid of a poem's actions reflects the juxtaposition of two imperatives: movement toward depletion and movement toward renewal. An enjambed line is an opportunity for multiple, even contradictory meanings in the hovering instant of line's end. Here expression arises from the reader's expectation either sustained or altered by the intrusive white space. Line manipulation affects syntax, momentum, spatial experience, connotation, and even cognitive resolution while it establishes controlling cadence. Once established as a normative length, the line is usually sustained in order to avoid violations offensive to either the ear or the eye that seeks symmetry, the imperative foremost to poetry.

This resistance to pattern breaking is so firm that any alteration of the expected order is regarded suspiciously. Readers balk at multiple caesuras, at arbitrary line breaks, at suspended or spatially dispersed parts of a single line, at breakage of words into syllables, etc. Such violations are common to free verse and may suggest a particular kind of voice selection, one different from the stable voice of metric form.

Perhaps the resistance to pattern breaking explains why some readers feel put off by an interrogatory line, which Warren has made a staple of his introspective lyric. He will ask questions in the full or partial line, usually in a tone indicative of emotional intensity, one that clearly risks control of the poem's moment as the line admits uncertainty, pauses, or turns the poem's motion. Successfully handled, the line gains the power of surprise, of aggression and rebalancing, of emphasis, and often enough shifts transmission of external information to internal information.

Many more specialized line forms occur in Warren's composition of his idiosyncratic rocking back and forth that is the systolic action of the mind and the diastolic action of the body. Among them might be mentioned the fulcrum line, for pivoting; a paratactic line used to build a visual, rhythmic, or physical moment of balance; the paradox line, which declares contradiction as truth-seeming; the tautological line, which circles; the staccato line, which impedes the reader; the command line, which intimidates; the ironic line, emphasizing the narrator's distance or expressing a strong attitude of difference from what he appears to say; the symbolic line, which subordinates declaration to connotation; and the metaphor line, carrying its figure of speech boldly.

Warren is a proven master of line scoring and variety, but certainly his lines are perceived by some ears as inflexible and clumsy. Few poems, if any, achieve quality and complexity if they do not integrate every sort of line. But types of lines may dominate a poem to the extent the poem seeks to tell a story of event and consequence, appreciate a scene, record information, or express the vital nature of an emotion. The individual and communal nature of lines establishes tone, by which we know what the writer thinks, and voice, the collective idiom through which the writer speaks.

Functions ordinarily define what a poetic line is. If lines historically manifested a metric measure, in modern poetry lines may represent a metric, sonic, or visual strategy. I think it would be hard for a line to hold less than the word or part of a word that occupies a vertical unit of space on a page of composition. A line typically possesses two or more syllables, as two syllables are required to make the smallest metric unit. A nonmetrical line could exist with any number of syllables.

Obviously the function of such minimal lines would also be minimal, a matter of account where the line's act is to carry information and to choreograph the rhythmic movement. The old argument over what constitutes a lyric and what a narrative poem seems, of late, reheated by theoretical criticism that holds all tales suspect and language itself, being plastic, manipulable, and historically calloused, deceptive in referentiality. Writing requires referentiality to link reader and writer. The poetic line transmits that referential information but, as I have said, carries as well a rhythmic guide-voice especially significant to lyric poems.

With a Warren lyric the staple line is not the conventional declarative but more insistently a violated, isolated, and roughly staccato line. It will resist a symmetric syllable count, will tend toward a clustered or "jammed" preponderance of stressed words, will extend a sinuous sentence over a number of lines and abruptly butt against it an equally rude short or half line, often enough interrupting with query, expostulation, or what I have heard called a wisdom statement, one that typically feels like a commentary unearned by and apart from the poem. The effect Warren seeks is that of a poetry so vital and surgent in energy it cannot be contained by conventions; it creates a boisterous colloquy. The effect of such language is power acquisition; we are meant to feel what is said can never be false, deceptive, or solipsistic. Nothing said is trivial. The will of this poetry defiantly emphasizes the cerebral and speculative action of the watching poet but so identifies it as a part of the manly action of his doing that even the static part of his nature becomes significant to the whole of living. The lines create immediacy, movement, for a form that is dominantly inactive, one that risks reader boredom without the illusion of character alteration and engagement.

But what can that mean? Warren has done nothing. The watcher is invented, a string of words only. And Audubon, evidence suggests, may well have fabricated all or part of his tale. If so, is this only much ado about nothing? I think it is more than that. *Audubon: A Vision* is an entertainment first, but an entertainment in the testing of moral response. Audubon does not actually kill the woman or her sons any more than he sleeps with them. He does not abuse their hospitality. He does not, as Ruppersberg seems to think, betray the nature he exists with. He does not flee in fear. But the woodspeople are dead; the regulators have gone; he is left with the burden of what he has and has not done, what he has and has not seen, what he knows and does not know, what the world is. He has a view of things, and a language is composed to express, indeed to embody that view. Once again we might imagine what we might have if Warren had done the poem in tidy couplets. And what if it were in elegiac quintets? Or in any form perfectly symmetrical and confidently continuous? One does not feel it could work any other way. But that is, perhaps, only because we have the poem as Warren made it, and this way is the brooding, male, violence-dreamed shape of the life that must have purpose or it is nightmare only. Warren has, that is to say, gambled, as all artists must, with a form that might create a living character.

Perhaps the most dazzling gamble in *Audubon: A Vision* is Warren's choice of an ending. Audubon dies in his bed, and time, which contains him, flows on; meaning continues, and contains the beautiful birds who "cry / In a tongue multitudinous, often like music." We seek to be equal to that. The ending is natural and follows the normal life story, even allowing for a certain blare of ripening gold light and drum roll of chill wind. Both the pastoral and the funeral elegy are served by Warren's celebration of the hero who goes before and redeems our best understanding. To know him, we see, is to know ourselves, a gesture of linkage that increases our sense of purpose in a world so visibly whirlpool-like. But Warren is too much the man here on this ground to leave his gaze on the outer world, however mythically reverberant, for the immediacy might be lost. Audubon's story is a man's life, and an event of crushing consequence in that life, and a life lived in the teeth of that event and all others. Is it not possible that any moment in any of our lives could have the same weight, hence the same grand beauty? Warren, in the closing poem, "Tell Me A Story," pleads for his own life story and for that singular life-defining moment, that fulcrum upon which meaning tilts.

Unlike the broken, grinding edges and wheezy, corrosive hinges of the lines in the first six sections, lines in this final unit are self-contained, syntactically complete, barely and slowly spilling one to the next, like a soothing fountain. The shortness and the spare jab of unmodified information create a sense of the essential, the final, and the dignified. This voice, one conceives, is capable of *knowing* what it asks for—time and distance and delight, all of which are aspects of *direction*, that which the great geese in naturalistic process already know. So we arrive at what Audubon came first to, his kinship—not a merger—with the geese in a world whose laws, knowledge or none, are inflexible and written before we have the first question to ask. But if we are like Audubon, and like the migrating geese, we are not them, are never to be them; nor are they us. Their fate is to go; our fate is to know, or try to know. And where we cannot truly know, we can and must seek the story, the shape of a life that might be lived, and in knowledge. James Olney writes that "In speaking of autobiography, one always feels that there is a great and present danger that the subject will slip away altogether, that it will vanish into thinnest air, leaving behind the perception that there is no such creature as autobiography and that there never has been."[19] But where there is no story of self, there is no self and no other. Worse, perhaps, there is no hope, no possibility of future life. If we are to exist, Warren's *Audubon* shows us, it must be in some manner like Audubon's life, but with consciousness alert, aware of the membrane between us and the rest, but testing its tensile strength. In telling our life stories, whether as confession or dramatic enactment, we are like James Weldon Johnson trying to get life right. The older a writer grows, the less concerned is he to make distinctions between his life and another's, and that, finally, may be the illuminating value of *Audubon*.

19. James Olney, "Autobiography and the Cultural Moment: A Thematic, Historical, and Bibliographical Introduction," in James Olney, ed., *Autobiography: Essays Theoretical and Critical* (Princeton University Press, 1980), 4.

The Poet and the Father

Robert Penn Warren and Thomas Jefferson

LEWIS P. SIMPSON

We hold these truths to be self-evident: that all men are created equal; that they are endowed by their creator with certain inalienable rights, that among these are life, liberty and the pursuit of happiness; that to secure these rights, governments are instituted among men, deriving their just powers from the consent of the governed; that whenever any form of government becomes destructive of these ends, it is the right of the people to alter or abolish it, and to institute new government, laying its foundation in such principles, and organizing its powers in such form, as to them shall seem most like to effect their safety and happiness.

Americans believe in the abstractions Thomas Jefferson wrote in that Philadelphia summer of 1776 and have died fighting for them, not only in the fateful struggle of colonials for freedom from the British Empire but in all the wars, declared and undeclared, they have since become engaged in.* Ironically, these include the wars, which lasted until 1890, to complete the dispossession of the native peoples who were on the land we call our own thousands of years before the first colonials appeared, plus a war or two in lands abroad influenced by our own imperial ambitions.

*This essay first appeared in *Sewanee Review* 104 (1996), 46–69. Copyright © 1996 by Lewis P. Simpson. Reprinted by permission of the editor.

Most ironically, the wars since the Revolution include one of the bloodiest wars in history—the one we waged against ourselves from 1861 to 1865: a war in which both sides claimed to be fighting for the sacred truths of the Declaration of Independence but were divided about the interpretation of the words in which these are stated, particularly the interpretation of the assertion that "all men are created equal." Yet in spite of this catastrophic disagreement, we yet regard the document authored by Thomas Jefferson—and ratified by the blood of the revolutionary army—as transcending all the ironies of our ever more complex history. At the same time we still consider the sacred truths proclaimed by the Declaration to have been incarnated in the commander of the revolutionary army and look upon General George Washington as the father of our country. More recently, in the long aftermath of our bitter Civil War, we have also developed—if not universally, almost so—a strong sense of parental regard for the martyred leader of the Unionist cause in this war, who, in 1863, created another sacred American text when he echoed the Declaration of Independence on the battlefield of Gettysburg.

Yet, while the Declaration of Independence is absolutely central to our history, we do not hold in veneration a definitive image of its author as a father figure. In our general conception, I think it is fair to say, Jefferson, in contrast to George Washington and Abraham Lincoln, is a somewhat remote, even ambivalent, presence, being accepted as a father figure more by the convention that confers this status on all the founders of the Republic than by reason of our attachment to him as an iconic presence.

This is not to say that Jefferson is not universally present to us. Perhaps he is too close to us, the interpretation of his ideas too intimately a part of our ongoing, often turbulent history—too intimately a part of our psychic makeup, of our everyday hopes and fears as individual Americans—for us to hold him up for veneration. Such a thought has often occurred to me, but in no way more insistently than in an effort over the years—not a notably successful effort I confess—to come to terms with one American poet's brooding involvement with the man who has been one of the most influential champions of freedom in modern history yet was a slave master all his long life. I have been particularly taken with the nature of this involvement as it is expressed in a long poem, the only poem of such length Robert Penn Warren wrote, *Brother to Dragons: A Tale in Verse and Voices*.

A singularly strange and daring work, this poem is made even stranger and more daring by the fact that thirty years after its first publication in 1953—after it had been republished in six editions and had begun to acquire the aura of a classic—it appeared in 1979, to use Warren's own words, in a "very different version" that is "in some important senses" a "new work."[1]

In the foreword to the new version of *Brother to Dragons* Warren suggests that even as the first version was published he was unhappy about the fact that, owing to "some confusion," the publisher had failed to employ the text incorporating all his revisions. But a desire to correct this confusion, as Warren acknowledges in the foreword to the 1979 version of the poem, was at best a secondary motive in his rewriting of the poem. Far from being a "patchwork reworking" of the first version, the second represents, Warren says, "a protracted and concentrated reliving of the whole process" of conceiving and writing the first version. We may, I think, interpret this statement to mean that the primary motive of *Brother to Dragons* II, as we may call it, is to be found in the poet's compulsion to return again and again to the question—poetic, philosophical, or it may be metaphysical—of his personal relation to Thomas Jefferson, especially as this was shaped by his knowledge of a lurid murder story associated with the region of Kentucky in which Warren was reared.

---

1. *Brother to Dragons: A Tale in Verse and Voices* (New York, 1979), xiii–xiv. Hereinafter this volume will be referred to as *BD* II, and *Brother to Dragons: A Tale in Verse and Voices* (New York, 1953) will be referred to as *BD* I in parenthetical references in the text. Both versions of the poem have been widely discussed. After making an extensive gathering of critical interpretations down to the early 1980s, James A. Grimshaw, Jr., concluded that his collection proves "there are indeed more than thirteen ways of looking at a blackbird." *Robert Penn Warren's "Brother to Dragons": A Discussion* (Baton Rouge, 1983), 10. Discussions subsequent to Grimshaw's collection support his conclusion. See especially the distinguished readings of the poem in John Burt, *Robert Penn Warren and American Idealism* (New Haven, 1988), 199–218; and Hugh Ruppersburg, *Robert Penn Warren and the American Imagination* (Athens, Ga., 1990), 38–78. Also, see the references to the poem in William Bedford Clark's valuable study focused on the Americanness of Warren, *The American Vision of Robert Penn Warren* (Lexington, Ky., 1991).

Known to Warren since boyhood in "garbled accounts," this story began in 1807, when Colonel Charles Lewis and his wife Lucy, a sister of Thomas Jefferson—together with their three sons and their three daughters—moved from the established world of Albemarle County, Virginia, to the frontier world of western Kentucky. Of some aristocratic pretension among the gentry of the Tidewater society, the Lewises presumably did not move by choice but were compelled by a pattern of hope that still urges Americans who have fallen on hard times to seek the promised land in the west. The leader of the Lewis family removal seems not to have been the father, Colonel Lewis, but two grown sons, Lilburne and Randolph. After the family arrived in Kentucky, it is not clear whether Colonel Lewis ever established himself on his own domain or not, but both Randolph (who does not figure in the murder story) and Lilburne bought parcels of land in Livingston County near the frontier town of Smithland and not far from the confluence of the Ohio and Cumberland Rivers. Lilburne chose a 1,500-acre site dominated by a bluff overlooking the Ohio. Here he erected what was for the time and place a rather grand house. Though in Kentucky his status was not, properly speaking, that of a planter but of a farmer, in the manner of the Tidewater planters he gave his house a name, "Rocky Hill." Assuming that Colonel Lewis did not buy his own property, Warren portrays Lilburne as presiding over something like a family dominion at Rocky Hill, the family consisting of his wife, Letitia, his parents, and the third brother, a somewhat feckless young man named Isham. (Warren leaves out the daughters in the Lewis family.) According both to the historical record and the poem, the Lewises were attended by several slaves, some of whom served as household servants, others as farm hands.

In contrast to the life the Lewises had known in Virginia, life at Rocky Hill was bleak. While they had not moved into a literal "wilderness," they had come to a community that had been established in a wilderness and still had a semiwilderness quality. Thus, although it is an interpretation that is not necessarily supported by the life of the actual Lilburne, Warren sees him as one who, coming to the "wilderness" as "a light-bringer" and "herald of civilization," yielded to a darkness engendered in him by the harsh life of the place he had come to.

Whether this is what happened or not, the historical Lilburne, for whatever reason, was moved by a dark impulse, when, on the night of December 15, 1811, the night before the first tremor of the New Madrid earthquake—the greatest recorded earthquake yet to occur on the North American continent—Lilburne commanded his slaves to gather in a cabin that served as the plantation kitchen (Warren calls it "the meat-house"). And here, in the terrified presence of the huddled slaves, aided by Isham, Lilburne literally butchered a seventeen-year-old male slave. Called George, his real name, in the first version of *Brothers to Dragons*, but for some unstated reason, called John in the second, the murdered slave was, as Warren describes him, "a sort of body-servant and handyman for Lilburne." George's death by the incredibly brutal act of the Lewis brothers was punishment for his having broken a pitcher prized by their mother, Lucy Jefferson Lewis, who had died a year earlier. Lilburne and Isham tried to hide their deed by having the slaves who witnessed it burn the body parts of George in the kitchen fireplace. But this disposal scheme was thwarted a few hours thereafter when the chimney of the fireplace collapsed onto the cabin during the first great tremors of the New Madrid quake. A second attempt to hide the murder by stuffing what was left of the flesh and bones of George in the masonry of a hastily rebuilt fireplace and chimney was confounded about two months later, when, as a result of the aftershocks of the New Madrid quake, the rebuilt chimney collapsed and George's remains were once again exposed. Additional grisly evidence came to light with the discovery not long after of George's head, which, unknown to Lilburne and Isham, had been carried off by a dog on the night of the murder. When the foul deed of Lilburne and Isham was revealed, they were arrested. (Slaves did not have the right to liberty and the pursuit of happiness, but they did have the right to life, at least in the sense that the law forbade their masters to murder them.) While on bail awaiting trial, the brothers concocted a scheme for a grand resolution of their predicament. According to the evidence set down in the legal record, they agreed to stand at their mother's grave and "present a gun at each others breast and fire at a word with an intention of killing each other" (*BD* I, 225n; *BD* II, 137n). But things went awry, when, as they prepared to fulfill their bizarre pact, Lilburne was accidentally killed. Unable to pull the trigger on himself, Isham fled. Soon caught, jailed, tried, and sentenced to death, he somehow managed to escape. His fate has never been known for certain, though it would appear that (as in Warren's poem) he eventually made his way to Louisiana, where he died in 1815 in the Battle of New Orleans.[2]

In *Brother to Dragons* Warren in general follows the recorded story of the Lewis family and the murder of John. Only one person in the poem has no basis in fact, an ancient black slave named Aunt Cat, who is depicted by Warren as having been Lilburne's nurse when he was a baby. Yet in its total configuration the "tale" Warren tells "in verse and voices" is an elaborate fiction, which, in addition to the persons already mentioned, includes not only two major historical figures—Thomas Jefferson and the explorer Meriwether Lewis—but a figure known only by the initials R.P.W., who is described as "the writer of this poem." Still another figure in the poem is R.P.W.'s eighty-year-old father. Adding to the bizarre quality of Warren's adaptation of the history of the Lewis family in Kentucky is the presentation of it as a ghost story. The only living characters in *Brother to Dragons* are R.P.W. and his father, and most of what happens in the poem occurs in a dimension beyond earthly time and place. Indeed Warren felt that he was assuming such a broad poetic license in

2. For a definitive historical account of the Lewis family, its relation to Thomas Jefferson, and the murder of the slave by Lilburne and Isham Lewis see Boynton Merrill, Jr., *Jefferson's Nephews: A Frontier Tragedy* (Princeton, N.J., 1976). Concerning *Brother to Dragons* Merrill comments "that in its unique literary and artistic quality it stands alone among other works based on the Lewis tragedy" (427). But Merrill indicates that he is not entirely in agreement with Warren's statement in the foreword to *BD* I that since he is "trying to write a poem and not a history," he has had "no compunction about tampering with facts." Warren has "succeeded admirably, both in his poem and in tampering with the facts," Merrill observes, though he adds that it may be "ventured that facts usually do stand in the way of poetic expression and artistic triumph, such as Warren has achieved." In the foreword to *BD* II Warren refers appreciatively to Merrill's "scholarly and conscientious account" of the history of the Lewis family and the murder of the slave by Lilburne and Isham Lewis. But he makes an indirect response to the ironic tone of Merrill's remarks about *BD* in the fillip to be found in the foreword to *BD* II (which was published three years after Merrill's book): a poem can "be totally accurate as history and still not be worth a dime as a poem" (*BD* II, xii–xiii).

his poem that he felt it appropriate to prefix an italicized notation to each of the two versions of *Brother to Dragons*, explaining that

> *The main body of the action lies in the remote past—in the earthly past of characters long dead—and now they meet at an unspecified place and unspecified time and try to make sense of the action in which they were involved. We may take them to appear and disappear as the urgencies of argument swell and subside. The place of this meeting is, we may say, "no place," and the time is "any time." This is but a way of saying that the issues that the characters here discuss are, in my view at least, a human constant.*

One complication in both the first and second versions of *Brother to Dragons* is the question of Warren's attitude toward the form of his poem. It gives the appearance of being a play. As Warren himself says in the prefatory matter to both versions, it is "a dialogue spoken by characters." Moreover, it has the initial apparatus we expect of a play text: a *dramatis personae* (or the equivalent): "THE SPEAKERS *in the order of their appearance*"; and a formal indication of the setting (or in this case, non-setting): "PLACE: *No place*; TIME: *Any time*." Yet, even though his poem may look like a play, Warren advises the reader, "it is not a play, and must not be taken as such."

Although Warren violated his own conception of his poem by preparing a stage version of *Brother to Dragons* that saw several productions on the noncommercial stage in the sixties and seventies, his advice to read *Brother to Dragons* as a poem is sound.[3] As the subtitle indicates, his chief intention was to write a poetic "tale in verse and voices" in which the voices are more important than the setting and in a sense constitute the setting.

The leading voices are those of the ghost of Jefferson and a living presence, R.P.W., who, though he appears in second place in the cast of characters, is the major voice in *Brother to Dragons*. Both Warren and a persona

---

3. For an excellent account of the dramatic productions of *BD* see Victor Strandberg, "*Brother to Dragons*: Poem / Play / Film," *Southern Quarterly* 33 (winter–spring 1995), 187–96. There is no published version of the play text. For the script of the television production see "*Brother to Dragons*: A Play in Two Acts," *Georgia Review* 30 (spring 1976), 65–138.

of Warren, R.P.W. is at times directly, at other times indirectly, the narrator of the tale, not only being present when he directly encounters the ghosts of Jefferson and others, but also being an assumed presence in all of their encounters with each other. It may not be too far fetched to say that R.P.W. is something like a Dantean presence in *Brother to Dragons*. A devoted student of Dante, Warren—like Dante when he wrote his great poem in verse and voices, the *Divina Commedia*—was in mid-life when he wrote *Brother to Dragons*, and the tale Warren tells is not unlike a journey through secular visions of hell and purgatory toward a vision, though muted, of salvation through the self's acceptance of responsibility for history.[4] But the Dantean reference of the poem is indistinct until its conclusion, when, as I shall suggest, it becomes quite significant. The more distinct frame of reference for *Brother to Dragons* is another poem in verse and voices. The source of Warren's title and to some degree the form of *Brother to Dragons*, this is the Book of Job. One of the "wisdom" books of the Old Testament, Job tells a tale in several voices of a righteous man who is in quest of the knowledge of why, when he has only "looked for good," evil has come to him; of why, when he has "waited for light," darkness has come. Job's search for the reason God has afflicted him represents a transformation of certain actual historical events into a tale that is fable and, in some ways, parable, but in the overall sense is a mythic record of an encounter between the soul, history, and the eternal. But unlike a New Testament book, which envisions history as a dimension of eternity, Job—ironically, like all the Old Testament, more "modern" than the New Testament—envisions eternity as a dimension of history. In *Brother to Dragons* a highly self-conscious modern poet imagines Job's story not as a direct source of the tale he wants to tell but as the shadowy

4. According to Joseph Blotner's biography of Warren, Warren's interest in Dante led him to begin a reading of the *Divina Commedia* in the original in the summer of 1939 during a month-long voyage to Italy on a tramp steamer. At that time he was devoting a great deal of time to completing a play he called "Proud Flesh." Based on the story of Huey Long, this work was partly in verse. Warren had no luck in getting the play published, let alone produced, but it was later transformed into his most successful novel, *All the King's Men*. The epigraph for this novel is a line from the third book of the *Purgatorio*. See Blotner, *Robert Penn Warren: A Biography* (New York, 1997), 176.

frame for his transformation of certain actual events that occurred in the time of the early American Republic into a myth about a ghostly Thomas Jefferson who finally surrenders his overweening pride in the intellectual capacity of man to direct his own destiny. Coming into the knowledge that man is by nature capable of evil as well as good, he accepts the limitations his Creator has imposed on his creation. The myth Warren imagines in *Brothers to Dragons* is the symbol, we may say, not of an encounter between the soul and history in the all-embracing dimension of eternity, but of an encounter in a placeless historical present between history and what has replaced the entity called "the soul," the entity whose will to power is idealized and proclaimed—if not directly, by powerful implication—in the Declaration of Independence: the autonomous secular individual or self.

The feature of the dark story of Jefferson's nephews that seems to have struck Warren most forcibly is that, in spite of all the research devoted to Jefferson's life and thought, no scholar has found a single mention of the murder anywhere in his voluminous writings, public or private, or discovered any record of his ever having mentioned it in conversation. Warren recognized that this apparent fact may at some time be proved to be untrue, but he was unconcerned about this possibility. As a poet, he said, he was interested in Jefferson's silence about the murder as symbolic truth, not as historical fact (See *BD* I, xi). What prompted Jefferson in effect to hide from himself a crime that was a matter of public knowledge? Was the author of the Declaration of Independence so blinded by the light of his delusionary belief in man's rational capacity to act on the basis of innate goodness that he was unable to face the innate capacity of man for acts of evil, especially when this capacity was demonstrated by his own flesh and blood? What would have been the significance to Jefferson himself and to his country had he recognized and tried to cope with the meaning of the murderous behavior of his own sister's children? The reason Warren eventually turned his hand to writing a second version of *Brother to Dragons* would appear to be that he more and more turned these questions inward. His search for the symbolic import of Jefferson's suppression of Lilburne's and Isham's savage deed becoming a symbol of his quest for his own meaning—not only as an American poet and an American citizen but as a self, a being, existing in history—Warren had no choice but to keep on living with and remaking the original *Brother to Dragons*.

I think I have by now indicated that an understanding of Warren's struggle to create the second version of *Brother to Dragons* demands more than the scrutiny of two texts for editorial revisions and textual emendations. Our attention may well be directed, for one thing, to the relation of both versions of the poem to other writings by Warren, especially writings prior to the composition of the first version. I think particularly, not of poems, but of a remarkable essay on Joseph Conrad's *Nostromo* Warren published two years before the first version of *Brother to Dragons* appeared. In spite of the tendency of critics to agree with Conrad's own evaluation of himself as "an imperfect aesthete" and "an imperfect philosopher," Warren argues in this deeply reflective essay that Conrad is to be defined "in the fullest sense of the term" as "a philosophical novelist." "Willing to go naked into the pit" over and over again "to make the same old struggle for his truth," Warren says, Conrad created in *Nostromo* "one of the few mastering visions of our historical moment and our historical lot."[5]

In placing a primary emphasis on the novelist as an individual—in asserting that Conrad created a "mastering" vision of the modern age out of the struggle "for *his truth*," for his own vision of history—Warren was seeking to delineate and to confirm his own literary motives as much as he was Conrad's. By the time he published his essay on Conrad, he had become a philosophical novelist in his own right. In no less than four distinguished novels—*Night Rider*, *At Heaven's Gate*, *All the King's Men*, and *World Enough and Time*—he had made his own struggle for visionary truth and had projected, if not a grand "mastering vision," a unifying vision of the American historical moment and the American historical lot—a vision centered in the perception that the underlying motive of American history is the fundamental motive Conrad had discerned in the history of the modern western world: the assertion of the connection be-

5. Robert Penn Warren, " 'The Great Mirage': Conrad and *Nostromo*," *Selected Essays* (New York, 1958), 31–58.

tween intellect and self-will. Foreshadowed in Western literature in the legend of Dr. Faustus and made plain in Marlowe and Shakespeare, this motive has often been expressed in stories, notably the tale of Prince Hamlet, that are symbolic embodiments of the self's struggle for identity in the context of the weakening of the traditional father-son relationship in a hierarchical society that had begun to yield to the revolutionary forces signified by what Sir Francis Bacon called "the advancement of knowledge." In Warren's first four novels the father-son relationship is viewed as it has existed under the historical circumstances of the culture of a nation that had hailed the victory of the modern conception of the autonomy of the self by, as Jefferson advocated, abolishing the law of primogeniture. An actor in the dialectical drama in the displacement in America of the traditional father-son relationship, the son in each novel discovers what Jack Burden in *All the King's Men* discovers: namely, that his only hope for salvation in his quest for self-identity is the recognition that he is a participant not only in the present but in the past, the past that includes the sins of his father. The implication is that if any sanity is to prevail in human relations under the governing terms of the redemptive promise offered by American history—the terms offered by the grand and noble, yet contradictory, equation between freedom and equality set forth by Jefferson in the Declaration—a dialectical tension between past and present, community and self, self and world, must somehow be maintained.

But under the terms of life in American society how can it be?

This question haunts Jeremiah Beaumont in *World Enough and Time*, the novel that followed *All the King's Men*. In Jeremiah's case the question has become not the identity of the son as opposed to that of the father but the question of the relationship between a self that seeks its identity in what is praiseworthy by society and a self that refuses any familial or social role, a self that declares the self to be its "own truth."[6]

If the tale of Jeremiah Beaumont represents a climax in Warren's depiction in his first four novels of the willful self as a central, and at times

---

6. Robert Penn Warren, *World Enough and Time: A Romantic Novel* (New York, 1950), 320.

destructive, force in American history, a deeper, more fundamental imagining of such a quest is suggested in the daring effort in *Brother to Dragons* to interpret the meaning of his own relationship to Jefferson, an effort that may be viewed as one climax in Warren's lifelong struggle to, like Conrad, envision our "historical moment and our historical lot."

We discover the governing focus of this struggle in the well-known dictum set forth in the foreword to the first *Brother to Dragons* and repeated in the foreword to the second: "Historical sense and poetic sense should not, in the end, be contradictory, for if poetry is the little myth we make, history is the big myth we live, and in our living, constantly remake" (*BD* I, xii; *BD* II, xiii). Or, to put this more directly, the historian is a poet and the poet is a historian; history is poetry and poetry is history, the historian being no less a maker than the poet, who in the original Greek meaning of the term for *poet* is one who makes. Living the big myth of history, Warren says in effect, the poet or the historian makes and remakes history through making and remaking the little myth of poetry.

With respect to the drama of making and remaking embodied in the two versions of *Brother to Dragons*, it is interesting that in the foreword to the first version of the poem Jefferson is referred to as "the spiritual father" of "American history." But in the foreword to the second version he becomes simply one who "helped to found" the nation (*BD* I, xi; *BD* II, xii). The implicit contrast between the image of Jefferson as the spiritual father of the nation and the nominal image of Jefferson as only one of the nation's founders clearly suggests that as Warren relived the first version of *Brother to Dragons* he had become less certain about the significance of Jefferson's role in American history. The result is a heightened tension in the second version of *Brother to Dragons* between Jefferson's identity in American history and the poet's sense of his own—his personal—historical identity.

We see this obliquely in the expanded interpretation—the "more significant role," as Warren puts it—of Meriwether Lewis in *Brother to Dragons* II (*BD* II, xiv).[7] Although he was a native of the former domain

7. In the foreword to *BD* II Warren associates the enlargement of the role of Meriwether with "the off-and-on process" of preparing the poem for the stage. This may have

of the family of Colonel Lewis, Albemarle County, Virginia, Meriwether
was not, as Warren says in the foreword to *Brother to Dragons* I, "the first
cousin of Lilburne and Isham Lewis." Warren rectifies this error in the
second version of the poem by referring to Meriwether simply as "the
cousin" of Lilburne and Isham. (He may in fact have been a distant one.)
In the second version of *Brother to Dragons* Warren is also more cautious
in his description of the relationship between Jefferson and Meriwether
Lewis, changing this from "cousin" to "kinsman." But, aware of the importance of kinship, however remote, in the society of the time and place,
Warren had no reason in the second version to change the description of
the relationship between Jefferson and Meriwether he had made in the
first. It was, he says, a "filial" relation (*BD* II, xiii).[8] In both versions, to
be sure, Warren implies another and stronger justification for the appointment of Meriwether to lead the expedition to explore the vast western territory the third president of the Republic had succeeded in adding to the
national dominion: it involved the trust a father might place in a son. If
in manipulating the Louisiana Purchase Jefferson had pursued tactics that
willfully defied his own conception of the proper limits of the constitu-
tional powers of his office, he justified his transgression of his own principles not primarily by the political, economic, and military importance of
bringing the western territory under the dominion of the new nation. The
Lewis and Clark Expedition was a climactic moment in a vivid desire
that, whether he was in office and out of office, ruled Jefferson all of his
life: the desire to illuminate the darkness of the world with rational
knowledge. He entrusted Meriwether not so much to head an official government expedition as to fulfill what was for him a compelling personal

given him the idea of heightening in *BD* II a dramatic relationship between Lilburne and
Meriwether that he apparently believed he had suggested in *BD* I. "Both Lilburne and
Meriwether Lewis" he says, "entered the wilderness as heralds of civilization, as 'light-
bringers,' and my story is about the difference with which they performed the role and their
tragic ends" (*BD* II, xiii). But the Lilburne-Meriwether relationship is not any more explicit
in the second version than in the first. One reason may be that the ghost of Lilburne in
both versions says very little, coming to us mostly through what others say about him, and
Meriwether says nothing about Lilburne.

8. See Merrill, *Jefferson's Nephews*, 211–12.

mission: that of bringing the vast Louisiana territory under the dominion of mind.

Two years following the completion of the Lewis and Clark Expedition, when, by Jefferson's appointment, he was serving as the governor of the Louisiana territory, Meriwether Lewis, at the age of thirty-five, died a violent death in the Tennessee wilderness while on a journey from St. Louis to the national capital. The circumstances were somewhat mysterious. One story is that he was murdered, but the more likely story is that, hounded by officials in Washington and unrespected by his subordinates, the "Governor of Louisiana, of all the West," as he ironically refers to himself in the poem, Meriwether fell into a state of extreme depression and took his own life (*BD* I, 182; *BD* II, 113). This was the story the historical Jefferson accepted, attributing Meriwether's suicide to "hypochondriacal affections."[9] In his enlarged role in the 1979 *Brother to Dragons* the ghost of Meriwether Lewis—whose brains, R.P.W. says, "Stare out like one great eye, \ Winking in blood"—becomes a crucial influence in the redemption of Jefferson from the ideology of the Enlightenment to what may be called the knowledge of the blood: the saving knowledge of that original and permanent stain of sin that entered the human blood stream when Cain murdered Abel (*BD* II, 109). Seeking a rational explanation for Meriwether's suicide, Jefferson's ghost says it resulted from Meriwether's being falsely accused of wrongdoing after his appointment to the territorial governorship. But, when he confronts the ghost of Jefferson in the climactic scene of *Brother to Dragons*, the ghost of Meriwether says that the truth is that he was "murdered" by Jefferson's "lies" about the goodness of human nature (*BD* I, 176–77; *BD* II, 109). When the ghost of Jefferson cries out, "No! no, my son!" the very exclamation is an admission of the truth of the accusation (*BD* II, 115).

Warren's basic conception of the relationship between Meriwether Lewis and Jefferson, which remains the same in both versions of *Brother to Dragons*, is hardly more significant than his conception, which also re-

9. See Jefferson's biographical sketch of Meriwether Lewis, *Writings of Thomas Jefferson*, ed. Andrew A. Lipscomb and Andrew Ellery Bergh (Washington, D.C., 1905) XVIII, 159–61.

mains the same in both versions, of the relationship between R.P.W. and the other nonghostly character in the poem, Warren's eighty-year-old father, Robert Franklin Warren. In the poem the father twice accompanies R.P.W. on visits to the town of Smithland, Kentucky, and the country thereabout, where the Lewises had settled. The first visit to the scene of the long-ago murder is based on actuality; the second would seem to be imagined. During the second visit Robert Franklin Warren tells R.P.W. about how his father (*i.e.*, Robert Penn Warren's paternal grandfather), with the return of spring each year, ritualistically administered to his sons a dose of bitter tonic made from the root of percoon and the bark of "prickly ash," the purpose being to "unthicken" their blood and make them less inclined to devilment:

> "Percoon, what's it like?" I said. And he: "Why, Son,
> It's just some sort of plant they called percoon."
> "But what's it like?" I said. And he: "Why, Son,
> I just don't recollect. But it's percoon."
> (*BD* I, 205; *BD* II, 127)

Although the real Robert Franklin Warren does not appear to have accepted Original Sin as doctrine, the poet uses his father as the voice for a folksy tale about a homemade tonic that may be taken as an ironic symbol of a truth beyond questioning, at least for many in the world in which his father had been reared, the blood knowledge of Original Sin. But R.P.W.'s natural father is conceived by the son, the maker of *Brother to Dragons*, as standing not in contrast to Jefferson, the sophisticated foe of king and priest and all emblems of what he considered to be superstition, but, in his folksiness, as a figure apposite to Jefferson. Both the living parental presence of the aged gentleman who rides to Smithland with his son and the ghostly presence of Thomas Jefferson haunt the poet's imagination of his parenthood. To him both the author of the great Declaration and the teller of the tale about the percoon are themselves poets—poets of a people who believe at once in original happiness and Original Sin, a people who are deeply and inextricably involved in the past yet believe they are free from the past. And the author of *Brother to Dragons*, explicitly in one case and by certain implication in the other, stands in a filial relation to both.

But the primary filial relation in *Brother to Dragons*, the one at the center of the poem, is the implied relation, that existing between R.P.W. (or Warren himself) and the historical Jefferson. In both versions of the poem Warren transforms what he takes to be the real Jefferson from a devotee of the Enlightenment into a lapsed philosophe who, in a ghost world, engages in a struggle for redemption from a terribly destructive innocence. Eventually, as Warren has it, the ghostly author of the Declaration of Independence—having through the agency of the living poet R.P.W. relived in the ghost world a part of his life that he refused to acknowledge in his earthly life—comes to the realization that his redemption is dependent on his acknowledgment of his intricate entanglement in the drama of good and evil that is human history. But, more importantly—in a way reminiscent of Jack Burden, the teller of the tale in *All the King's Men*—R.P.W., in his involvement with the story of Jefferson, is telling the story of his own quest as a twentieth-century American poet for a redeeming vision of the meaning of history.

It is not, I think, an incidental fact that Warren finally managed to complete and publish the second version of *Brother to Dragons* during a period when his poetic output was at its height, a time when, I remember, Cleanth Brooks remarked to me, "Red is writing poems by the yard." A year after he published the second version, Warren published a collection of striking lyrical poems written in the short span of three years, 1977–1980. Bearing the significant title *Being Here*, this volume concludes in an unusual way with an appended prose notation, entitled "Afterthought," in which Warren says that, representing "a fusion of fiction and fact in varying degrees and perspectives," the poems herein collected constitute "a shadowy autobiography." He does not suggest what may be fiction, what may be fact in the poems, saying only that as a question may be more significant than the answer, "fiction may often be more deeply significant than fact." "Indeed," he adds, "it may be said that our lives are our own supreme fiction."[10]

10. Robert Penn Warren, *Being Here* (New York, 1980), 107–08.

"Our lives are our own supreme fiction": in effect in the "After-thought" to *Being Here* Warren recognizes that his writings, early and late, bear the tangible, if not always distinct, imprint of a lyrical, a deeply subjective, motive.

The imprint of the subjective motive is plain in a certain ambiguity in the setting Warren seeks to establish for *Brother to Dragons*. In both versions it is clear that Warren conceives the setting, No place, Any time, to be a way of getting a perspective on Our place, Our time. It is not quite so clear that in a more subjective sense Warren conceives the setting to be My place, My time. The setting, in other words, is not a metaphysical beyond but the historical context of the poet's life during the time of the composition, and recomposition, of his poem, this being the time of the greatest crisis in our national identity since the Civil War: the agonizing epoch that began in the American response to North Korea's invasion of South Korea and reached a climax in the disastrous historical trap of the misadventure in Vietnam but, as daily events unmistakably indicate, has yet to reach its historical culmination.

The setting becomes explicit in R.P.W.'s meditation on the prosperity of Smithland when he returns for his second visit to the community associated with the long-ago crime of Lilburne and Isham. In *Brother to Dragons* I, and also in *Brother to Dragons* II, with a few nonessential changes, this reads,

> And paint is on the house, and new stores,
> And gas pumps are a rash that's worse than measles.
> And Ford and Plymouth vie to make you happy,
> And money jingles in the local jeans.
> That's fine. I don't begrudge such solvency,
> And who's to blame if there is some correlation
> Between it and the dark audit of blood
> In some Korean bunker, at the midnight concussion?
> Yes, who's to blame? For in the great bookkeeping
> Of History, what ledger has balanced yet?
> And every entry is a scrawl of blood.
>
> (*BD* I, 206; *BD* II, 127)

The ultimate rationale in the making and remaking of *Brother to Dragons*, it may be suggested, lies in Warren's need to resolve his vexatious sense of the connection between his own identity and the identity of the poet who, in writing the Declaration of Independence, became the maker, the father, of the American Republic, and so of all American poets since. Responding to the ironic feeling of alienation from the standard image of Jefferson as the man of reason, Warren attempted to transcend his ironic reservations about the Jefferson of historical fact by creating a fictional Jefferson he could identify with, a Jefferson immanent in his (Warren's) imagination of his own historical moment. The attempt to create this Jefferson was bold not because it involved the device of imagining the present in terms of a ghostly world beyond time and place. It was bold in that, although he may not have yet set it down in explicit formulation, Warren followed the dictum stated in *Being Here* that one's own life is the supreme fiction one lives. In the making and remaking of *Brother to Dragons*, he attempted nothing less, you might say, than to incorporate the supreme fiction that was Jefferson's life into the supreme fiction that was his own life—to fuse the Jefferson of historical fact and a fiction of *his* redemption with the fact of the historical R.P.W. (or the poet himself) and a fiction of *his* redemption. Whether or not the poet is successful in this endeavor depends on how convincing we deem it to be.

In their final appearances in the poem, Meriwether says, "All is redeemed, In knowledge," and Jefferson responds,

> But knowledge is the most powerful cost.
> It is the bitter bread.
> I have eaten the bitter bread.
> In joy, would end.
>
> (*BD* II, 120)

But do we believe the ghost of Jefferson will indeed end in joy? Do we believe that the ghostly Jefferson, having eaten of the bitter bread of knowledge, has truly transcended the bitterness of the knowledge the earthly Jefferson hid from himself? This question receives an answer as R.P.W.—in "the last light of December's, and the day's, declension" (*BD*

II, 130)—contemplates the meaning of his final leave-taking from the site on the bluff of the river where Lilburne had built his house and where he and Isham had committed the heinous act the historical Jefferson could not hide from the world but could and did hide from himself. R.P.W.'s thoughts become a meditation on the nature of joy when (in both versions of *Brother to Dragons*) they lead to the addition of an intimate personal dimension to the poem:

> And I think of another bluff and another river.
> I think of snow on brown leaves, and below
> How cold and far was light on a northern river,
> And I think of how her mouth and mine together
> Were cold on the first kiss. We kissed in the cold
> Logic of hope and need.
>
> Who is to name delusion when the flesh shakes?
>
> So in this other year by another river,
> Far in Kentucky there, I raised my eyes
> And thought of the track a man may make through Time,
> And how the hither-coming never knows the hence-going.
> Since then I have made new acquaintance
> With snow and brown leaves.
> Since then I have made new acquaintance
> With the nature of joy.

Continuing his meditation, R.P.W. thinks "of the dead beneath my feet" and

> Of Lilburne on his mountain here,
> Who brought no light into the dark, and so died.
> And of another mountain, far away,
> In Albemarle, where Lilburne's kinsman sleeps,
> And thought of all
> Who had come down the great river and are
> Nameless. What if
> We know the names of the niggers hunkering by the wall,
> Moaning? For yes, we know each name,

The age, the sex, the price, from the executor,
Who listed all to satisfy the court.

(*BD* II, 129–30; *cf. BD* I, 208–12)

R.P.W. thinks too of other things we know: "all the names who went with Meriwether / To lie on night-mats in rain, and hear the utterance of ocean." This knowledge, together with the knowledge embodied in his recollection of a transforming moment in his own life, is the immediate reference for the basic question R.P.W. thereupon propounds about the relation between knowledge and redemption. "But what is knowledge / Without the intrinsic mediation of the heart?"

Although he has never returned to the scene of the long-ago murder, R.P.W. says at the end of *Brother to Dragons* that he has held this "land-scape in his heart" ever since he "crossed the evening barnlot, opened / The sagging gate," prepared "To go into the world of action and lia-bility."

I had long lived in the world of action and liability.
But now I passed the gate into a world

Sweeter than hope in that confirmation of late light.

(*BD* II, 130, 132)[11]

It would seem that in the conclusion of *Brother to Dragons* Warren's reference is no longer to the Book of Job but to the *Divina Commedia*, es-pecially the conclusion. His vision of a world sweeter than hope echoes Dante's imagination of his passage from the state of hope in the *Purgato-rio* into the state depicted in the *Paradiso*. As would be expected in the case

11. *Cf. BD* I. In *BD* II the stanzaic pattern is altered, and the last four lines of *BD* I (quoted below) are cut:

I walked down to the car where my father had been waiting.
He woke from his cold drowse, and yawned, and said,
"You finished what you climbed up there for, Son?"
And I said: "Yes, I've finished. Let's go home."

As is the case in the cutting of various other lines that appear in *BD* I, the elimination of these lines would seem to have been done for the sake of poetic economy and force.

of a poet who assumes the metaphysical tradition of Christianity, the poet of the *Divina Commedia* finds that his imagination fails him utterly in the presence of the vision that comes to him at the end of his journey, when his love for his spiritual guide, Beatrice, is transformed by a vision of the unity of the triadic God. To describe the ineffable, transcendent state of consciousness, beyond history and beyond imaging as a world his vision represented, was not, the poet says, "a flight for my wings: / Except that my mind was struck by a flash / In which what it desired came to it." In this flash he knows that his "desire" and his will are "being turned like a wheel, all at one speed, / By the love which moves the sun and the other stars."[12]

What R.P.W. says at the end of *Brother to Dragons* obviously strikes a more consoling note in the breast than Jack Burden's austere statement at the end of *All the King's Men* about going "out of history into history and the awful responsibility of Time." Certainly R.P.W.'s valedictory is far more consoling than the terrifying question Jeremiah Beaumont leaves dangling before the reader at the end of *World Enough and Time*, "Was all for naught?" Yet, we may ask, is the resolution of the story of Jefferson and R.P.W. and their involvement in the murderous act of Lilburne and Isham Lewis effectively resolved in R.P.W.'s vision of passing into "a world / Sweeter than hope"? At best this is an uncertain image. Is not the image of a world "sweeter than hope" self-contradictory? Is it a world at all? For all his long struggle with *Brother to Dragons*, Warren's conclusion to the second version—although more economically and sharply presented than in the first version—does not truly transcend the ironic sense of history and human nature that pervades the poem. Nor, as indicated

12. Robert Penn Warren, *All the King's Men*, Bantam Edition (New York, 1980), 438; *World Enough and Time*, 512; Dante, *The Divine Comedy*, trans. C. H. Sisson (Chicago, 1981), 498. *Cf.* the epigraph for *All the King's Men*, which is from the second book of the *Divina Commedia* (the *Purgatorio*): "Mentre che la speranza ha fior del verde" ("As long as hope has any touch of green"). The treatment of hope in *BD* lends credence to the interpretation that the setting of *BD* is in some sense a vision of Hell, Purgatory, and Paradise. (*Cf.* n3 above.) Like the experience of Jack Burden, who in *All the King's Men* is in a way the persona of Warren, R.P.W.'s experience in *BD* bears an ironic relation to a spiritual journey for which Dante provides the archetype.

in R.P.W.'s comment immediately preceding his vision of a world "sweeter than hope," does Warren intend for us to think so.

> We have yearned in the heart for some identification
> With the glory of the human heart. We have devised
> Evil in the heart, and pondered the nature of virtue.
> We have stumbled into the act of justice, and caught,
> Only from the tail of the eye, the flicker
> Of joy, like a wing-flash in thicket.
>
> (*BD* II, 131)

In the ironic echo of the Dantean moment of transcendent vision of joy, we realize that the sense of irony that pervades *Brother to Dragons* tempers the effort of the poet to imagine a world sweeter than hope. We may think of the dragons in *Brother to Dragons* as pride, especially intellectual pride, and the other deadly sins, but in sum there would seem to be one dragon, the dragon of self—the desiring, willing self. I would not at all make Warren out to be a Freudian, but there is strong suggestion in his vision of the later Freud's depiction of structure of the self (libido, ego, and superego) of the tragic opposition that exists between the ego and the ruthless superego. This situation in the Freudian concept of human nature is not treatable by analysis, the alienation of the ego and the superego being permanent, having no remedy whatsoever. Some such sense of the irremediable nature of the human condition haunts the tale of R.P.W.'s quest for his historical self-identity in his dramatic encounter with the ghosts he summons from the history of the time of the making of the nation.

That this is the case is pinpointed in the change of one word in the second part of *Brother to Dragons* II. The ghost of Jefferson speaks to R.P.W.:

> I have long since come to the considered conclusion
> That love, all kinds, is but a mask
> To hide the brute face of fact,
> And that fact is the un-uprootable ferocity of self. Even
>
> The face of love beneath your face at the first
> Definitive delight—even that—

> Is but a mirror
> For your own ferocity—a mirror blurred with breath,
> And slicked and slimed with love—
> And even then, through the interstices and gouts
> Of the hypocritical moisture, cold eyes spy out
> From the mirror's cold heart, and thus,
> Self spies on self
> In that unsummerable arctic of the human lot.
>
> (*BD* II, 33)

Compare the last line of the passage I have just quoted with the last line in the same passage in the 1953 poem, in which we read, "In that unsummerable arctic [not of 'the human lot' but] of the human alienation" (*BD* I, 47). The term "human alienation" suggests that the self somehow recognizes its compulsion to seek its own aggrandizement at the expense of all other selves and therefore conceivably has some control over its behavior; in substituting the term "human lot" in the second version Warren has his ghostly author of the Declaration of Independence conceiving the isolate condition of the self as absolute and beyond alleviation. Since Warren weighed each word with great care in his revision of *Brother to Dragons*, we would appear to be justified in saying that his depiction of the ferocity of the self is more intense in the second version. But in either version it is sufficiently intense—is it not?—to cast the shadow of a dark question over the theme of redemption in *Brother to Dragons*: After such an austere and forbidding vision of the demonic nature of the self, what redemption for Jefferson, for Lilburne, for Meriwether, for R.P.W.? Or for their creator, the poet Robert Penn Warren?[13] Concluding with R.P.W.'s vision of "a world / Sweeter than hope," does not the poem end in ironic ambiguity?

Yet, paradoxically, in the ambiguous resolution of the redemptive—

---

13. In the foreword to both editions Warren says poetry, being "more than fantasy," is obligated to try to "say something about the human condition" (*BD* I, xii; *BD* II, xiii). In changing the term "human alienation" to "human lot" Warren may be said to conform more strictly to his general vision of poetry in relation to history.

which is to say, the autobiographical—motive in *Brother to Dragons* lies the success of this singular poem, for it opens up an instructive vision of considerable scope and power.

The ghostly Jefferson's frightening meditation on love and the "unuprootable ferocity of the self" is not only a metaphor of the fate of the self under the specific conditions of American history. In the larger sense Warren's effort to interpret the meaning of the silence of the philosopher and poet who wrote the Declaration of Independence about a murder committed by his nephews assumes the character of an ironic metaphor of the character of the self in modern history generally. Signifying the complicity between self and the modern power of secular mind, it represents a psychic situation Marlowe and Shakespeare intuited; Francis Bacon, although without quite realizing what he was doing, set forth in *The Advancement of Learning* and elsewhere; and John Donne, the most sophisticated English poet and intellectual of his age, explicitly delineated in 1611 in his poem "Anatomy of the World":

> And new philosophy calls all in doubt. . . .
> Prince, subject, father, son, are things forgot,
> For every man alone thinks he hath got
> To be a phoenix, and that then can be
> None of that kind, of which he is, but he.[14]

Donne saw that in willfully identifying itself with the greatly enhanced powers of the rational intellect that were coming into play in the age of Francis Bacon, the modern self would identify itself with the mind of God and increasingly seek to assume a preemptive role in history. Perhaps we may conceive Donne's vision in the early seventeenth century of the destruction of the traditional father and son relationship as foreshadowing its fulfillment in a visionary manifesto by a late eighteenth-century American philosopher, poet, and slave master, proclaiming all men to be free and equal. Perhaps we may even take Donne's vision to foreshadow the twentieth-century American poet, novelist, and historian who would

14. Donne, "An Anatomy of the World," *Major British Writers* (New York, 1959), I, 383.

struggle for half his literary life to write an interpretation of the anatomy of the Jeffersonian world, a world that he saw as reaching a culmination in his own world—our own world—a world representing at once the triumph of the Jeffersonian faith in the union of the human will and the human intellect and the most violent period in human history. Whatever else we may learn from Warren's long pursuit of his relationship to Thomas Jefferson, we discover that we are not done with Jefferson and that Jefferson most assuredly is not done with us.

Robert Penn Warren and the "New Paradigm"
A Case Study of the Birds

VICTOR STRANDBERG

When I went to Japan several years ago to teach American literature at Kobe College, I was uncertain what the curriculum would be, so
I thought I could best cover all contingencies by bringing with me the
most recent *Norton Anthology of American Literature* (4th ed., 1994), on the
theory that Norton editions of anything figure to be the best in the business. In Japan, a casual perusal of the book left my high esteem for it in-
tact until I turned to the anthology's section on Robert Penn Warren's
poetry to begin formulating some ideas, and it was at this point that I encountered what I am calling the New Paradigm—a term that I realize
may sustain a variety of definitions.

In the context that I am describing, the New Paradigm is a term of
reproach for inadequate or even irresponsible scholarship, and reproach
most specifically for the theory of criticism that lies behind the inadequate
and/or irresponsible performance. What raised the red flag for me was the
assertion by the Norton editors that Warren's career as a "major" poet
"began" with the publication of *Audubon* in 1969, when the poet was in
his mid-sixties. A closer look revealed that the only poems published in
the *Norton Anthology* were in fact those that appeared after its 1969 time
marker. Even more remarkably, neither the editorial introduction nor the
book's bibliography even mentioned a title of any Warren volume before

1968 (except for one passing mention of *Promises*).[1] The injustice thus inflicted on Warren's earlier career will be obvious to anyone familiar with the whole range of his poetry, but let me render a short roll call of major works thereby cast into oblivion: *Promises*, good enough to win the Pulitzer Prize in 1957 but not good enough to register with Warren's "Major Poetry," it would seem; *Selected Poems* (1944), the fruition of a quarter century of creativity, reaching from the poet's youth into early middle age; *You, Emperors, and Others* (1960), the book that closed out the most dramatic development in Warren's verse, the identity crisis involving the persona he calls "you"; and *Tale of Time* (1966), with its unforgettable entries occasioned by the death of the poet's mother.

In fact, one cannot begin to give a meaningful account of Robert Penn Warren as a poet without touching upon certain crucial works that date back to his beginnings: "Kentucky Mountain Farm" and "The Return: An Elegy," in his first volume, *Thirty-Six Poems* (1935); the longer entries in *Eleven Poems on the Same Theme* (1942); "The Ballad of Billie Potts," the most crucial single poem in all Warren's poetry (1943); "Ballad of a Sweet Dream of Peace" in *Promises* (1956); the "Mortmain" sequence on the death of his father in *You, Emperors, and Others* (1960); and the title sequence, "Tale of Time," along with the "Delight" sequence in *Tale of Time* (1966). And, capping off the list, an adequate sampling of Warren's major poetry would have to include a page or two of the best poetry in *Brother to Dragons*—perhaps the Minotaur segment or the coming of the annus mirabilis. Underscoring the "major" importance of these works is the fact that, two years before the 1969 time marker when (the Norton editors say) Warren "began" to publish his "Major Poetry," Warren was awarded the highest honor an American poet could receive, the Bollingen Prize for Poetry.

Clearly, something was badly wrong with the *Norton Anthology*'s judg-

---

1. *The Norton Anthology of American Literature*, 4th ed., vol. 2 (New York: W. W. Norton, 1994). The Robert Penn Warren entry occupies pp. 2396–409; the bibliography for these pages is on p. 2857. The previous (third) edition of this anthology, dated 1989, is identical to the fourth edition with regard to the Warren entries. For a review of Warren's pre-1969 poetry, the Norton editors recommend the *Selected Poems* of 1985—an anorexically thin sampling, as any serious review of the subject quickly makes evident.

ment about what constitutes Warren's "major" poetry—a mishap that now raises doubts in my mind about its reliability with writers that I do not know so well. Regarding Robert Penn Warren, the question I could not understand during my visit to Japan was how, with an abundance of scholarship available, the Norton editors could consign so much of Warren's major poetic achievement into oblivion. Eventually a suspicion crossed my mind. For the first time, I consulted the *Norton Anthology*'s bibliography at the back of the book, and there my suspicion was confirmed: the editors mentioned only a single book-length study in their bibliography, declaring this work "the best book" on Warren's poetry. That one privileged work of criticism applies its subtitle, "Robert Penn Warren's Major Poetry," solely to Warren's poetry from 1969 onward, as follows: "[Warren's] greatness as a writer [of poetry] . . . began with *Audubon: A Vision* (1969)." This critic is entitled to have his opinion, of course, but we are entitled to wonder why so greatly arguable a thesis gains exclusive rights in the *Norton Anthology*, whose opening commentary on Warren reads as follows: "In 1969 . . . Robert Penn Warren published his long poem, *Audubon: A Vision*, the book which announced that here was a major poet."[2] So far as the *Norton Anthology* is concerned, that one critic's opinion appears to have decided the issue of what is worth reprinting from Warren's six decades as a poet, with the result that thousands of the anthology's users around the world will consider only the final one-fourth of Warren's poetic career worthy of their attention.

I must confess a private interest in this argument. My book *The Poetic Vision of Robert Penn Warren* (1977) covers the whole career of Robert Penn Warren up into *Now and Then* in 1976, and I do admit to some puzzlement about being totally excised from the scholarly record in the Norton bibliography, along with other writers of book-length studies whose existence is not acknowledged, such as Floyd Watkins and Randolph Runyon. But the larger issue is the truncation of Warren's poetic career. It is

2. Calvin Bedient's book *In the Heart's Last Kingdom: Robert Penn Warren's Major Poetry* (Cambridge, Mass.: Harvard University Press, 1984) is the only book-length study mentioned in the *Norton Anthology*'s bibliography. The only other entries for scholarship are a collection of interviews and two essay collections, edited by Harold Bloom and William Bedford Clark.

as though one could appreciate T. S. Eliot only by way of *Four Quartets*—with "Prufrock, "The Waste Land," "The Hollow Men," and *Ash Wednesday* shucked off as "minor" entries—or, to follow the lead of the *Norton Anthology*, not mentioned at all. Or one might say it is like approaching Wordsworth only through *The Prelude*, with the Lucy poems, "Tintern Abbey," and the "Intimations Ode" designated as literally not worthy of being mentioned.

In suggesting that a New Paradigm of literary criticism lies behind this short-changing of Warren's achievement as a poet, I shall take a moment to mark three mileposts in my education in this subject. My first serious doubt about our most prestigious publishing houses occurred years ago when I talked with the first and greatest historian of the Holocaust, Raoul Hilberg, whose magisterial *The Destruction of the European Jews* was about to be reissued in a revised, three-volume edition. He had been thinking of using a university press, he told me, until he noticed that some bad books about the Holocaust were coming off the Harvard, Yale, Princeton, and Oxford presses. Finally, when—in his words, and with his emphasis—"an *unbelievably* bad book" came off the University of Princeton Press, he went back to a commercial publisher.

My second milepost of illumination about the New Paradigm was a book by a noted feminist scholar who gained wide approval for her contention that Nathaniel Hawthorne's high reputation was the result of a patriarchal conspiracy that puffed his work because of his male gender while suppressing more worthwhile books by contemporary women.[3] My colleague Buford Jones, a lifelong scholar of Hawthorne, points out in rebuttal that Hawthorne's reputation was established during his decade of total anonymity, when reviewers like John Neal and John Greenleaf Whittier praised his stories without any inkling as to whether the writer was a man or a woman.

My third milepost was a book that I reviewed, *Creating Faulkner's Reputation*, which claimed that Faulkner's popularity was engineered by a

---

3. See Jane Tompkins' chapter 1, "Masterpiece Theater: The Politics of Hawthorne's Literary Reputation," in *Sensational Designs: The Cultural Work of American Fiction, 1790–1860* (Oxford and New York: Oxford University Press, 1985).

cabal of Southern conservatives and New York Jewish intellectuals (led by Robert Penn Warren, Allen Tate, and Irving Howe) who were looking for a front man to propagate conservative values wherewith to fight the Cold War.[4] Although admirable scholarship fills this book with regard to publishing statistics and background correspondence, the writer in his nearly three hundred pages never once considers the possibility that the excellence of Faulkner's writing might have some bearing on his reputation. Nor does he show any awareness of Faulkner's subversion of "conservative, Cold War values"—in *The Wild Palms*, for example, concerning family values (his heroine deserts her children and gets an abortion); in *The Bear* and *Requiem for a Nun* concerning capitalist rapacity (some of these pages seem lifted directly from *The Communist Manifesto*); and in *Light in August* and *Go Down, Moses* concerning racial justice. (Jean-Paul Sartre, the violently anti-American French Marxist who actually created Faulkner's reputation by contriving to get him the Nobel Prize in 1950, would be deeply indignant, I think, to find himself exposed as a purveyor of conservative, Cold War values.)

I put the *Norton Anthology*'s maltreatment of Warren's poetic career in the same category as the above offenses. We live in an age when violations of critical due process are justified, we are told, by the larger context of social needs—the need to upgrade the status of nineteenth-century women writers, in the case of Hawthorne; the need to expose the conspiracy that perpetrated Cold War values, in the case of Faulkner; and the need (as best I can figure it out) to inflate the literary values of the present time over those of the past in the case of Robert Penn Warren—supporting, that is to say, the Provincialism of the Present Moment.

---

4. Lawrence H. Schwartz, *Creating Faulkner's Reputation: The Politics of Modern Literary Criticism* (Knoxville: University of Tennessee Press, 1988), pp. 4 and 5: "Faulkner was seen [by his promoters] to exemplify the same values that Western intellectuals saw in capitalism which made it morally superior to communism. . . . Had anti-Communism not become prevalent, Faulkner could not have achieved renown." Contrary to Schwartz's thesis, Faulkner scholars generally acknowledge that Faulkner's reputation—in academe, most notably—soared to the heights only after he won the Nobel Prize in 1950, an event engineered in large measure by prominent European intellectuals, the most prominent of whom was Jean-Paul Sartre.

Although it is always a debatable issue to pinpoint the beginning of a New Paradigm, I believe a reasonable candidate for that designation in American literary criticism is Fredric Jameson's essay, "Metacommentary," which won the Modern Language Association prize for 1971 as its best essay of the year. A professor of French who reacted bitterly (it would seem) to the failure of the May 1968 student uprising in Paris, Professor Jameson with this essay brought his program of Marxist revolution into American academe, in the hope that a new generation would adopt its precepts. And his first precept is to reject categorically the traditional bourgeois notion of literary value. "In our time," his first sentence states with satisfaction, "exegesis, interpetation, commentary have fallen into disrepute."[5] The reason for this welcome development, Jameson claims, is that now, thanks to Critical Theory, the work of art stands exposed as a reprehensible instrument for capitalist exploitation of the reader: "its mechanisms function as a censorship whose task is to forestall any conscious realization on the part of the subject [*i.e.,* the reader] of his own impoverishment; and to prevent him from drawing any practical conclusions as to the causes for that impoverishment and mutilation, and as to their origin in the social system itself" (122).

For our purposes, the most interesting item in the essay is Jameson's specific condemnation of the New Criticism for perpetrating corrupt literary values (please do remember, regarding the following citation, that this essay was declared the best of the year by the Modern Language Association): "thus the concept of a symbol . . . along with the other basic components of the new-critical ideology such as irony and point of view . . . all too often encourages the most irresponsible interpretation of an ethical or mythical and religious character. . . . No wonder we feel symbolism in the novel to be such a lie: no wonder Williams' attack on metaphor came as a liberation to a whole generation of American poets!"

5. Fredric Jameson, "Metacommentary," *PMLA* 86, no. 1 (1971), reprinted in *Contemporary Literary Criticism: Modernism Through Post-Structuralism*, ed. Robert Con Davis (White Plains, N.Y.: Longmans, 1986), 112.

(112).[6] A bit later, Jameson reveals what has replaced symbol and metaphor as a preferable literary practice. "And let us also mention here," he says, "that ultimate opposition of metaphor to metonymy, codified by Roman Jakobson, and similarly adopted by Lacan to describe the psychic forces" (119).

So far as Warren's reputation is concerned, I believe Jameson's preference for metonymy over metaphor provides the key for understanding the *Norton Anthology*'s attitude. Disseminated through the power of our literary elite, for example the Yale English department, the vogue of metonymy can sometimes prove to be a wonderfully convenient literary fashion. Among the possible definitions of the term, let us consider the oldest and simplest definition: metonymy is the use of a part to represent the whole, as in "All hands on deck." If you can consider a part to represent the whole, there is no need to go through the vast labor of studying Faulkner's novels by way of analyzing his literary reputation: some letters between Allen Tate and Irving Howe could be all we need. So, too, why bother to investigate Hawthorne's tortuous path to fame during his anonymous years, when a patriarchal conspiracy might explain his success in a more socially useful fashion? In the case of Robert Penn Warren, I would say that to render his career exclusively through the prism of his last years is an instance of metonymy, as it is commonly employed by the New Paradigm. Which is to say, if a part represents the whole, why bother yourself with the first half century of the poet's career in designating his "Major Poetry"?

Fredric Jameson's purpose in giving preference to metonymy over metaphor was avowedly political. Whereas metaphor is a mere surface feature in Jameson's judgment—an "epiphenomenon" that reflects only the internal design of a poem or novel—metonymy implies the "deep

---

6. Jameson does not say in this passage whether it was Raymond Williams or William Carlos Williams who attacked metaphor, but if it was William Carlos Williams, Jameson is wrong: Williams famously hoped "through metaphor/to reconcile the people and the stones" in "A Sort of Song." On the other hand, if Jameson was thinking of Raymond Williams, it is hard to imagine how he managed to liberate a whole generation of American poets.

structure" of the thing, which is its role as an agent for oppressive social forces such as "late capitalism," sexism, racism, homophobia, and the like. Metaphor (Jameson says)—along with other literary devices like irony and point of view—disguises the ways by which literature propagates those social evils; metonymy unmasks them. Jameson's opinions were not, of course, consciously in the minds of the Norton editors who slighted Warren's verse, but after Jameson's anointing by the Modern Language Association, this New Paradigm of criticism did come to pervade the profession of literature at elite levels, inevitably affecting our most prestigious publishing houses. Moreover, the temptation to metonymize a poet's career need not have a political purpose: the gain of professional advantage or convenience has been a sufficient motive, I would judge, in many cases. And so we cannot be too surprised if Warren's "Major Poetry" turns out to be only that which got sifted through the Provincialism of the Present Moment.

Within that provincialism, the idea of binary opposites, such as that between metonymy and metaphor, is one of the phoniest, most condescending theories to come out of the Critical Theory movement. Radical politics aside, *both* metonymy and metaphor are useful figures for the artist at work, and they need not be regarded as acting in opposition. But between metaphor and metonymy, I have to admit that I favor metaphor. A major reason for this preference is, avoiding the Provincialism of the Present Moment, the classical standard: metaphor is attested by millennia of testimony. Four centuries before Christ, Aristotle, in *The Poetics* (chapter 22), said that the greatest thing by far, for the poet, is to be a master of metaphor; it is the truest sign of original genius, a gift that cannot be learned from others. Our great poets in English—Chaucer, Shakespeare, Donne, Milton—have obviously verified Aristotle's statement, and Robert Frost, in "The Constant Symbol," went so far as to say that "Poetry is nothing but metaphor. Every poem is a new metaphor inside or it is nothing." I propose to indicate, through tracing the evolution of one master metaphor, how much is lost in the metonymizing of Warren's poetic ouevre.

*   *   *

In its rendition of Warren's "Major Poetry," all of it dated from 1969, the *Norton Anthology* includes the following lyric ("Tell Me a Story") from the conclusion of *Audubon*:

> Long ago, in Kentucky, I, a boy, stood
> By a dirt road, in first dark, and heard
> The great geese hoot northward.
>
> I could not see them, there being no moon
> And the stars sparse. I heard them.
>
> I did not know what was happening in my heart.
>
> It was the season before the elderberry blooms,
> Therefore they were going north.
>
> The sound was passing northward.

Clearly, this poem poses a geographical riddle: why does the poet insist on three repetitions of the birds' northward direction? Since he "could not see them," but only "heard them," why does it matter what direction they are flying? Would the birds' music not stir the boy's heart equally well if they flew east, west, south, or anywhere? In the end, the answer to this question bears out T. S. Eliot's observation, apropos of Shakespeare, that to know any of his work really well, you have to know all of it. Which is to say, the New Paradigm's philosophy of metonymy, using one stage of a poet's career to stand in for the whole profile, will not do. Quite the contrary, the geese flying northward in *Audubon* are explicable only in the light of Warren's whole ouevre, including some of his fiction, in whose light it turns out that the northward direction is very significant.

When we do survey all of Warren's poetry, we find that the geographical riddle in question extends a thread of meaning from the wild geese of the poet's sixties to the following lines written by the same poet at about age seventeen (*ca.* 1922, unpublished):

> As, delicate within the stone,
> Pick-steel divulges to the view
> The printed frond that once had grown
> Greener—but perfect now as new:

So had disaster's bluntless stroke
Cracked the heart-stone and there revealed
Within the stone the stone that spoke
Of ferned shade and summer's field.

This poem appears to be the earliest literary expression of Warren's life-long obsession with the Fall from Innocence: his persona's "heart-stone," ossified by the world's suffering, cracks open to reveal a fossilized lost paradise ("ferned shade and summer's field"). Although teenagers sometimes exaggerate their hardships, Warren's personal suffering, even at age seventeen, certainly sufficed to motivate such a poem. Two years earlier, the fifteen-year-old Warren had lost an eye to a stone thrown by his brother, a mishap that led to a suicide attempt at college—perhaps about the time of this poem.

One effect of this deeply felt trauma—the Fall into a ruined world—was a series of bird images (usually a hawk) that kept reappearing throughout Warren's lifetime as a poet. Typically soaring into the sunset as its earthbound alter ego looks up enviously from the gathering darkness, these birds represent the Jungian psychodrama of the lost anima, the ideal prelapsarian self that flies away when the Fall happens, leaving an empty husk of self behind. Two such images, cited from poems a half century apart, will illustrate the lifelong persistence of the trope:

The sunset hawk now rides
The tall light up the climbing deep of air.
. . . .
His gold eyes scan
The crumpled shade on gorge and crest
And streams that creep and disappear, appear,
Past fingered ridges and their shrivelling span.
("Kentucky Mountain Farm," Part VI, "Watershed," 1928)

In Warren's *Selected Poems* of 1975, "Evening Hawk" makes unmistakably clear the Jungian role of this creature:

Look! look! he is climbing the last light
Who knows neither time nor error, and under

Whose eye, unforgiving, the world, unforgiven, swings
Into shadow.

In the fallen world down below, which is altogether given over to time
and error, the narrator of this poem can "hear . . . history / Drip in darkness like a leaking pipe in the cellar." And in his final volume, the *Selected
Poems* of 1985, the octogenarian poet repeats the trope yet again in "Mortal Limit"—a title that points toward his own imminent death. "I saw the
hawk ride updraft in the sunset over Wyoming," the first line reads, taking the poem toward a question: "Beyond what range will gold eyes see /
New ranges rise to mark a last scrawl of light?"

The lifelong recurrence of these bird images makes it clear that our
answer to the geographical puzzle in *Audubon* requires a careful examina-
tion of the anima psychology behind them. And that objective, in turn,
requires some knowledge of the writer's earlier literary biography. The
fact that Warren began writing *Audubon* at the end of World War II gives
us a clue as to the dense matrix of creativity out of which the poem finally
bloomed a quarter of a century later. World War II was in fact the true
period of Warren's emergence as a Major New Original writer, in all
three realms of poetry, fiction, and criticism. In criticism, as James Justus
has written, Warren's hundred-page major opus on Coleridge's *The Rime
of the Ancient Mariner* laid bare the fable of guilt and expiation that Warren was transmuting into his own major theme of a lifetime—a theme
that even Audubon (the character) enacts as he ponders how his display
of a gold watch brought about the woman's crime and execution. In fiction, the war years saw the publication of three masterly novels, *Night
Rider* (1939), *At Heaven's Gate* (1943), and *All the King's Men* (written between 1939 and 1946)—a novel that now appears certain to claim perma-
nence as an American classic alongside such titles as *Huckleberry Finn* and
The Great Gatsby. In poetry, the Provincialism of the Present Moment to
the contrary, Warren's emergence as a major American poet occurred
with the publication, in 1942 and 1943, of *Eleven Poems on the Same Theme*
and its companion masterpiece, "The Ballad of Billie Potts." (For convenience, we shall call them the Twelve Poems.) These powerful, utterly
original poems, in turn, set the stage for their successor a decade later,

Brother to Dragons (1953)—an American epic poem of a status comparable to Whitman's *Song of Myself* and Hart Crane's *The Bridge*.[7] The major reason why the Twelve Poems actually marked the emergence of Warren as a major poet lies, needless to say, in their combination of artistic mastery and prophetic power. It was here, in these poems, that Warren's anima psychology found its most compelling expression. But it should not surprise anyone that these poems also represent a rich crossfertilization with Warren's greatest novel, which he was writing during these same wartime years. Although space does not permit an extensive exegesis of these correlations, a few of the more important ones may suggest how Warren's undeniable emergence as a major fiction writer in *All the King's Men* paralleled his emergence as a major poet in the Twelve Poems.

First, the theme of lost innocence is the "Same Theme" of the *Eleven Poems on the Same Theme* and "The Ballad of Billie Potts," with the persona of "you" serving the same role as Jack Burden in the novel—that is, the role of the Humpty Dumpty figure whose fall from innocence cannot be repaired even by all the king's men. The novel's postlapsarian motifs show up everywhere in the Twelve Poems. Jack Burden's general experience of alienation appears in the poem "Monologue at Midnight," for example, and in particular his broken relationship with his mother correlates with the filial guilt of the poem "Revelation":

> Because he had spoken harshly to his mother,
>
> . . . .
> The peacock screamed . . .
>
> . . . .
> And the owl's brain glowed like a coal in the grove's combustible dark.

Similarly, Jack's shame over his decrepit "father," Ellis Burden, correlates with that of "you" toward the shabby grandfather fingering the wen on

---

7. Thanks to the Provincialism of the Present Moment, the original (1953) version of *Brother to Dragons* is no longer in print. The revised (1979) version was also out of print until Louisiana State University Press offered a reprint in its Voices of the South series (Baton Rouge, 1996). The failure of the *Norton Anthology* even to mention its title may be a clue as to how such a major opus can find a path to oblivion.

his forehead in the poem "Original Sin: A Short Story." Jack's escape into the distraction of politics parallels that of the political fanatics in the poem "Terror" who are swept up by the appeal of Franco, Hitler, Mussolini, and Stalin. So too is Jack's flight to California like the escape to Florida in the poem "Pursuit," where "you simply need a change of scene." Jack's turn toward determinism to escape responsibility in the Great Twitch episode correlates with the same motif in the poem "Crime," where the psychotic murderer blamelessly "cannot seem / To remember what it was he buried under the leaves." And Jack Burden's search for innocence in the fetal, underwater state is reflected in the water imagery of "End of Season," where "waters wash our guilt and dance in the sun." Even the elegant, archaic style of the Cass Mastern episode finds a correlative in "Love's Parable," a baroquely worded poem that, like Cass Mastern's confession, moves away from the "sore / Of self that cankers at the bone" towards a final expiation—the "testaments / That men, by prayer, have mastered grace." And what was once the most widely anthologized of the Twelve Poems, "Bearded Oaks," correlates with the most intractable of all postlapsarian motifs in Warren's novel, the existential question of annihilation. "Bearded Oaks," that is to say, describes the state of being dead by comparing it to being under water:

> Passion and slaughter, ruth, decay
> Descend, minutely whispering down,
> Silted down swaying streams, to lay
> Foundation for our voicelessness.
>
> All our debate is voiceless here,
> As all our rage, the rage of stone;
> If hope is hopeless, then fearless fear,
> And history is thus undone.

For Jack Burden, the equivalent sense of history being undone comes through the metaphor of a baseball game that evokes the most pessimistic idea in the history of human thought, the idea of entropy bringing on the final extinction of the entire universe: "After the death of Judge Irwin . . . I felt that a story was over. . . . But if anything is certain it is that no story

is ever over, for the story which we think is over is only a chapter in a
story which will not be over, and it isn't the game that is over, it is just an
inning, and that game has a lot more than nine innings. When the game
stops it will be called on account of darkness. But it is a long day" (355,
first paragraph of chapter 9).

In counterpoint with these postlapsarian motifs, the Fall from Innocence also evokes memories of the lost paradise in both the Twelve Poems
and the novel. Paralleling Jack Burden's lost paradise—his youthful romance with Anne Stanton—is the romance in the poem "Picnic Remembered," and what follows the broken romance in both the poem and the
novel is an explicit extension of Warren's bird imagery into the region of
Jungian psychology. That is to say, the hawk soaring in the last light of
day here represents the Jungian anima, or ideal self, flying away from the
fallen self trapped down below in earthbound darkness. The poem "Picnic Remembered" renders this anima metaphor by way of a question:

> Or is the soul a hawk that, fled
> On glimmering wings past vision's path,
> Reflects the last gleam to us here
> Though sun is sunk and darkness near?

In the chapter of *All the King's Men* that parallels "Picnic Remembered"
(chapter 7), Warren's anima/bird metaphor comes into play through Anne
Stanton's love songs. "Oh, Jackie-Boy, oh Jackie-Bird, it's a wonderful
night, a wonderful night," she sings to him, making a pun on his name
(Bird/Burden) before turning the motif into a nursery rhyme appropriate
to the theme of primal innocence: "Poor Jackie-Bird, he is a pest, but I'll
rock him to sleep in a soft warm nest, and I'll sing a song to Jackie-Bird,
the sweetest song he ever heard, poor Jackie-Bird, poor Jackie-Bird. . . .
I'll never let anything hurt poor Jackie-Bird."[8] In the end, as we know,
she does let something hurt poor Jackie-Bird, very badly, through her own
affair with Willie Stark, but even before that great trauma, Jack Burden
ruefully ponders "the years that had gone by since the summer when we

---

8. Robert Penn Warren, *All the King's Men* (Harcourt Brace Jovanovich, 1984), 287.

sat in the roadster and she sang to Jackie-Bird, and promised to never let anybody hurt poor Jackie-Bird. Well, she kept her promise, all right, for Jackie-Bird had flown away that summer, before the fall came, to some place with a better climate where nobody would ever hurt him, and he had never come back. At least, I had never seen him since" (323). Jackie-Bird's flight to a place with a better climate is an obvious anima image evocative of those sunset hawks we saw earlier from the first and last Warren volumes. But Jackie-Bird also points ahead some thirty years to "Heart of Autumn," the closing poem of *Now and Then* (1978), where the birds in the sunset turn out to be wild geese similar to those heard by the boy at the end of *Audubon*. Here, in "Heart of Autumn," however, the fall has indeed come, and the birds are not flying north but south, to "a land of warm water." There is no doubt that the anima psychology that we observed in "Picnic Remembered" and *All the King's Men* extends crucially into this poem of three decades later, because the speaker contrives through his imagination to leave his autumnal world behind and join the birds in their migration back toward paradise:

> and I stand, my face lifted now skyward,
> Hearing the high beat, my arms outstretched in the tingling
> Process of transformation, and soon tough legs,
>
> With folded feet, trail in the sounding vacuum of passage,
> And my heart is impacted with a fierce impulse
> To unwordable utterance—
> Toward sunset, at a great height.

If Jackie-Bird in *All the King's Men* and the geese in this poem ("Heart of Autumn") represent the anima escaping southward, what does it mean that at the end of *Audubon* the geese are flying north, as the boy states three times? The flight north means the return of the anima rather than its departure. That is why the last line of *Audubon* is "Tell me a story of deep delight." The return of the anima *is* a story of deep delight, its joy making possible a reversal, if only for the duration of the epiphany, of the syndrome of man's fall. Perhaps all the king's men cannot put Humpty together again, but the world's beauty can do so, restoring the

Warren persona to his lost paradise at least for the moment at the end of *Audubon*. During this moment, he enjoys the anima-state of being perfectly happy to be exactly who he is, living in the world just as it is. That is why he says, "I did not know what was happening in my heart."

Now that we have correlated Jackie-Bird's flight in *All the King's Men* (in 1946) with the geese flying south in "Heart of Autumn" (in 1977), and now that we have contrasted those two motifs with the geese flying north in *Audubon* (in 1969), one final bird metaphor will complete this brief overview of Warren's anima psychology. Before *Audubon*, there was one earlier instance of wild geese flying north, reversing the syndrome of man's fall, and that occurred at the end of the single most crucial poem that marked Warren's emergence as a major poet, "The Ballad of Billie Potts" (1943). Here the "you" gains redemption from the fall not through recovering some spurious lost "innocence" but by joining the procession of wild creatures that make up "the one life we all live":

> under the stars, pure in its clamorous toil,
> The goose hoots north where the starlit marshes are.
> The salmon heaves at the fall, and, wanderer, you
> Heave at the great fall of Time. . . .
>
> .   .   .   .
>
> Brother to pinion and the pious fin that cleave
> The innocence of air and the disinfectant flood
>
> .   .   .   .
>
> Back [to]
>
> .   .   .   .
>
> The itch and humble promise which is home.

The return of the anima in this poem, when "the goose hoots north" instead of escaping southward, correlates with the Warren persona's calm acceptance of mortality, the universal heritage of death shared by all the creatures moving "homeward"—to eternity—at the end of "The Ballad of Billie Potts": "Back to the silence . . . back / To the high pool, motionless, and the unmurmuring dream." The Warren persona comes in the end to kneel "in the sacramental silence of evening" awaiting the father's fatal hatchet blow. This scene of reconciliation with the fallen world ranks with the grandest achievements in all of Warren's writing, combining intense visionary and aesthetic power to mark the unmistakable emergence of a Major Poet in American literature.

The crosshatch of references I have made, covering a span of fifty to sixty years, indicates the damage inflicted upon the poet's oeuvre by the metonymic approach to scholarship. Moreover, important as it is, Warren's anima psychology represents just one section of his Wagnerian-scale bird orchestra, whose total ornithology probably rivals that of John James Audubon himself. Beginning with the blue jay, cardinal, and "sunset hawk" that are given prominence in "Kentucky Mountain Farm," along with the two undertaker-buzzards of "Pondy Woods," Warren has filled his poems with prominent roles for crows, eagles, hawks, owls, sea gulls, meadowlarks, mockingbirds, whippoorwills, cormorants, herons, bullbats, orioles, redwing blackbirds, pheasants, flycatchers, wild geese, kestrels, grackles, sparrows, swallows, thrushes, warblers, ospreys, jorees, and flamingos. As a closing instance of what he can do with just one of these creatures, let us consider the metaphor that Warren construes from two owl calls that reply to one another despite being separated by some thirty years and the Atlantic ocean. The owl of the present moment is in Italy; the one from the past in Kentucky (the "home-dark" of the poem):

> This small owl calls from the moat now.
> The other owl answers him
> Across all the years and miles that
> Are the only Truth I have learned.
> And back from the present owl-call
>
> . . . .
>   the reply
> Of a dew-damp and downy lost throat spills
> To quaver from that home-dark,
> And frame between owl-call and owl-call
> Life's bright parenthesis.
> ("In Italian They Call the Bird *Civetta*," *You, Emperors*, 1960)

That closing metaphor about two owl calls enclosing "Life's bright parenthesis" indicates exactly why this poet's career must not be metonymized:

to subordinate the pre-1969 poetry is to leave us, metaphorically speaking, with only one owl call, thereby raising the question: of what use is a single parenthesis? One owl call does answer another across the range of Warren's poetry, with respect to a vast variety of motifs, and it is a reckless mode of criticism to eradicate the earlier voices from the poetic record. No critic can hope to exhaust the entire web of meanings afforded by Robert Penn Warren's poetic ouevre or even exhaust the one entry in the web represented by Warren's elaborate symbolism of the birds. The problem with metonymy, in the sense of using the last part of his career in place of the whole, is precisely its injustice to metaphor, the career-long evolution of a texture of meanings in which each part illuminates the others. The *Norton Anthology*'s false dichotomy between major and minor, using 1969 as the demarcation point, breaks the woof and web of Warren's poetic achievement in a finally irresponsible way.

This essay has, in effect, been an argument against the misuse of a single word. If the *Norton Anthology*'s one favored critic had used the subtitle "Robert Penn Warren's Late Poetry," instead of "Major Poetry," I would not have had the occasion to write this paper. But his phrase "The Major Poetry" creates one of those binary oppositions that Critical Theory supposedly finds reprehensible when they are lodged in the mass mind of the bourgeoisie. In this case, the binary opposition polarizes Major and Minor, poetry that is Important versus that which is Not Worth Our Time. No one who knows Warren's entire poetic oeuvre can—or would want to— allow this binary opposition to go unchallenged. I do acknowlege, of course, that any scholar may publish any opinion he can get a publisher to print: that is not the issue. What is the issue is the mysterious way by which such an opinion, no matter how debatable, gets anointed as God's Truth by so prestigious a publisher as W. W. Norton, which additionally excludes from its bibliography virtually all mention of either competing scholarship or even competing (pre-1969) volumes of poetry by one of our great poets.

    With respect to Robert Penn Warren's poetry, the *Norton Anthology* is not the worst in the business. That distinction is reserved to the Macmillan *Anthology of American Literature* (George McMichael, general editor), whose fifth edition (1993) never mentions the name of America's first Poet Laureate in the index to its 4000-plus pages. But we do expect the highest standards from the *Norton Anthology*, and the record shows a decline in its standards after the mid-1980s. Working backward through time, we find that the third edition of the *Norton Anthology* (1989) is identical to the fourth edition (1994) with regard to the Warren entries—that is, only what comes after 1969 matters. The second edition (1985), by contrast, at least mentions the title *Brother to Dragons*, which is excised from the later editions apparently in deference to the assertion of its one privileged scholar that Warren's "Major Poetry" only "began" with *Audubon* in 1969. Prior to that scholar's influence, the second edition also includes two of Warren's important earlier poems, "Bearded Oaks" and "Picnic Remembered," which were cited from the volume that actually announced the arrival of a major new poet, *Eleven Poems on the Same Theme* (1942).[9]

I think it significant that the mishandling of Warren's poetic oeuvre in the *Norton Anthology* is matched by its mishandling of scholarship about Warren. Apart from their single uniquely privileged scholar, the *Norton Anthology*'s only other entries for scholarship are one collection of interviews and two essay collections, a total of three books which conveniently shield their one consultant from any sustained, unified competing arguments. This paucity of references forms an interesting contrast to the anthology by Perkins, Bradley, Beatty, and Long, *The American Tradition in Literature* (7th ed., vol. 2, McGraw-Hill, 1990). The latter volume devotes only three pages to Warren's verse, compared to the *Norton Anthology*'s thirteen pages, but in those three pages it reflects the whole chronological range of Warren's oeuvre, with an early poem ("History Among the Rocks," 1935); one from the poet's middle period ("Founding Fathers, Nineteenth-Century Style, Southeast U.S.A.," 1957); and a later entry ("Blow, West Wind," 1966). They also, in these three pages, find the space to list all of Robert Penn Warren's published books, and they further list,

---

9. The first edition of the *Norton Anthology* (1979), published in the same decade as Warren, Brooks, and Lewis' own magnificent *American Literature: The Makers and the Making* (1973), gave no space at all to their rival anthologist, whom they apparently designated as too "minor" a poet to deserve even a mention, although Warren had already won two Pulitzer Prizes and the Bollingen Prize for his poetry.

without either favor or prejudice, all sixteen books of scholarship about Robert Penn Warren published since 1958. (Norton's list of four scholarly books goes back only to 1982.)

Until the Norton editors show better judgment, anyone interested in avoiding the Provincialism of the Present Moment might well consider using the Perkins, Bradley anthology of American literature. Ironically, the finest anthology ever published, by common consensus, was Warren's own *American Literature: The Makers and the Making* (New York: St. Martin's Press, 1974), coedited by Cleanth Brooks and R. W. B. Lewis. While we lament its totally unjustified demise, anthology users would be well advised to consider the status of Warren's oeuvre as an index to judge the integrity of all such publications. So long as the New Paradigm and its aftermath continue to shortchange Warren's achievement, we can only expect his reputation to undergo continued attenuation. The judgment of the birds calls for resistance to that iniquity when we see it.

Founding Director of the United States Civil War Center, DAVID MADDEN is Donald and Velvia Crumbley Professor of Creative Writing at LSU. Among his eight scholarly works are *Wright Morris, Harlequin's Stick, Charlie's Cane,* and *The Poetic Image in Six Genres.* His edited works include *American Dreams, American Nightmares; Tough Guy Writers of the Thirties; Classics of Civil War Fiction* (with Peggy Bach); and works on Nathanael West and James Agee, and he has edited innovative literature textbooks. Short story writer, poet, and playwright, he has published ten novels, the latest of which is *Sharpshooter,* set during the Civil War.

JAMES H. JUSTUS is Professor Emeritus of English at Indiana University, Bloomington. He is the author of *The Achievement of Robert Penn Warren,* the first full-length study of Warren's life and work.

R. W. B. LEWIS directed the American Studies Program at Yale. He is the author of *The American Adam* and *Edith Wharton,* which won the Pulitzer Prize for biography, and coeditor with Nancy Lewis of *The Letters of Edith Wharton.*

C. VANN WOODWARD's *The Burden of Southern History* is in its third edition. Sterling Professor of History Emeritus at Yale University, he won the Pulitzer Prize for history in 1982 for *Mary Chestnut's Civil War. Origins of the New South, 1877–1913* won the Bancroft Prize. He was a member of the American Academy of Arts and Literature and the American Academy of Arts and Science. He died in 1999.

T. R. HUMMER is Professor of English at Virginia Commonwealth University. His books of poetry are *Walt Whitman in Hell; The 18,000-Ton Olympic Dream; Lower-Class Heresy; The Passion of the Right-Angled Man;*

The Angelic Orders, and *Translation of Light.* He won the 1999 Hanes Prize for Poetry.

JOHN BURT is a poet and professor of English at Brandeis University. His works of poetry are *Work Without Hope* and *The Way Down.* He is the author of *Robert Penn Warren and American Idealism,* and he is the editor of *The Collected Poems of Robert Penn Warren.* He is literary executor for Robert Penn Warren. His work in progress deals with the Lincoln-Douglas debates.

ERNEST SUAREZ is Associate Professor and Chair of the English department at Catholic University of America. He is the author of *James Dickey and the Politics of Canon: Assessing the Savage Ideal; Southbound: Interviews with Contemporary Southern Poets;* and *Discover a New Stand: Southern Poetry from 1950 to 2000.* He has published numerous articles on major American poets.

DEBORAH WILSON is Associate Professor of English and director of the Master of Liberal Arts program at Arkansas Tech University. She has published numerous articles on American writers and is working on a book about Gayl Jones.

LUCY FERRISS is Associate Professor of English and Creative Writing at Hamilton College. She is the author of four novels, *Against Gravity, The Gated River, Philip's Girl,* and *The Misconceiver,* and the critical study *Sleeping With the Boss: Female Subjectivity and Narrative Pattern in Robert Penn Warren.*

JAMES A. GRIMSHAW, JR., is Regents Professor at Texas A&M University System in Commerce. He is the author of *Robert Penn Warren/Cleanth Brooks: Friends of Their Youth* and *Robert Penn Warren: A Descriptive Bibliography, 1922–1979.* He has edited several books on Warren, including *Cleanth Brooks and Robert Penn Warren: A Literary Correspondence* and *Robert Penn Warren's "Brother to Dragons": A Discussion.* He recently coedited *Robert Penn Warren's "All the King's Men": Three Stage Versions* with James A. Perkins.

Lewis P. Simpson is Boyd Professor Emeritus at Louisiana State University. He coedited the *Southern Review,* second series, from 1965 to 1987. He is the author of *The Brazen Face of History, The Dispossessed Garden, The Man of Letters in New England and the South,* and *The Fable of the Southern Writer.* He is editor of several books, including *The Federalist Literary Mind.*

Dave Smith is Boyd Professor and coeditor of the *Southern Review* at Louisiana State University. Among his numerous books of poetry are *Floating on Solitude, Tremble, Fate's Kite, Cumberland Station,* and *The Wick of Memory: New and Selected Poems, 1974–2000.* He is the author of *Onliness,* a novel, and of five books of criticism.

Victor Strandberg is Professor of English at Duke University and author of *Greek Mind/Jewish Soul: The Conflicted Art of Cynthia Ozick; The Poetic Vision of Robert Penn Warren; Religious Psychology in American Literature: The Relevance of William James;* and *A Faulkner Overview.*

INDEX